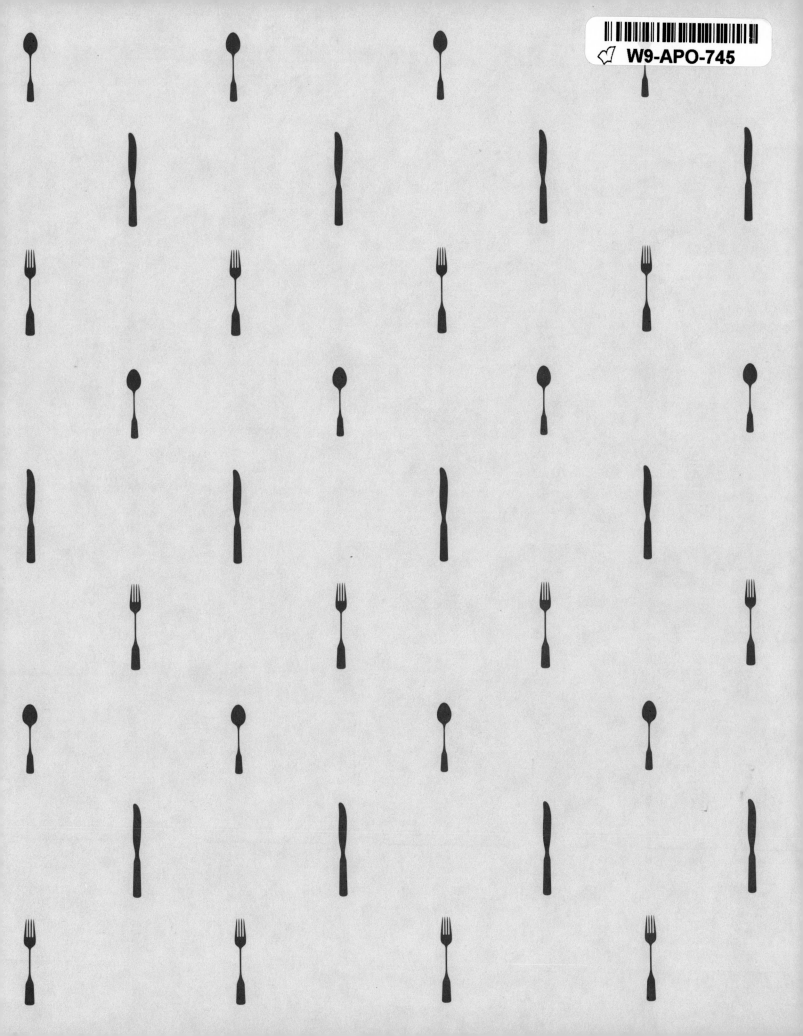

Fresh Ways
with Desserts

Time-Life Books Inc.
is a wholly owned subsidiary of
TIME INCORPORATED

FOUNDER: Henry R. Luce 1898-1967

Editor-in-Chief: Henry Anatole Grunwald
Chairman and Chief Executive Officer: J. Richard Munro
President and Chief Operating Officer: N. J. Nicholas Jr.
Chairman of the Executive Committee:
Ralph P. Davidson
Corporate Editor: Ray Cave
Group Vice President, Books: Reginald K. Brack Jr.
Vice President, Books: George Artandi

TIME-LIFE BOOKS INC.

EDITOR: George Constable
Director of Design: Louis Klein
Director of Editorial Resources: Phyllis K. Wise
Acting Text Director: Ellen Phillips
Editorial Board: Russell B. Adams Jr., Dale M. Brown,
Roberta Conlan, Thomas H. Flaherty, Donia Ann Steele,
Rosalind Stubenberg, Kit van Tulleken,
Henry Woodhead
Director of Photography and Research:
John Conrad Weiser

PRESIDENT: Reginald K. Brack Jr.
Executive Vice Presidents: John M. Fahey Jr.,
Christopher T. Linen
Senior Vice Presidents: James L. Mercer,
Leopoldo Toralballa
Vice Presidents: Stephen L. Bair, Ralph J. Cuomo,
Terence J. Furlong, Neal Goff, Stephen L. Goldstein,
Juanita T. James, Hallett Johnson III, Robert H. Smith,
Paul R. Stewart
Director of Production Services: Robert J. Passantino

Editorial Operations
Copy Chief: Diane Ullius
Editorial Operations: Caroline A. Boubin (manager)
Production: Celia Beattie
Quality Control: James J. Cox (director)
Library: Louise D. Forstall

Correspondents: Elisabeth Kraemer-Singh (Bonn);
Maria Vincenza Aloisi (Paris); Ann Natanson (Rome).

Library of Congress Cataloguing in Publication Data
Main entry under title:
Fresh ways with desserts.
  (Healthy home cooking)
  Includes index.
  1. Desserts. 2. Desserts — Composition.
I. Time-Life Books. II. Series.
TX773.F73 1987   641.8'6   86-14528
ISBN 0-8094-5828-4
ISBN 0-8094-5829-2 (lib. bdg.)

For information on and a full description of any Time-Life Books
series, please write:
Reader Information
Time-Life Books
541 North Fairbanks Court
Chicago, Illinois 60611

Time-Life Books Inc. offers a wide range of fine recordings,
including a *Big Bands* series. For subscription information, call
1-800-621-7026, or write TIME-LIFE MUSIC, Time & Life Building,
Chicago, Illinois 60611.

COVER
*Ready to be spooned up, a frozen peach
dessert captures the color and luscious taste of
the ripe summer fruit. A touch of brown sugar,
vanilla and almond extract adds flavor to this
creamy confection, which comes to 193 calories
a serving (recipe, page 59).*

HEALTHY HOME COOKING

SERIES DIRECTOR: Dale M. Brown
Deputy Editor: Barbara Fleming
Series Administrator: Elise Ritter Gibson
Designer: Herbert H. Quarmby
Assistant Designer: Elissa E. Baldwin
Picture Editor: Sally Collins
Photographer: Renée Comet
Text Editor: Allan Fallow
Editorial Assistant: Rebecca C. Christoffersen

Editorial Staff for *Fresh Ways with Desserts:*
Book Manager: Barbara Sause
Associate Picture Editor: Scarlet Cheng
Researcher/Writers: Jean Getlein, Henry Grossi
Copy Coordinators: Elizabeth Graham,
Ruth Baja Williams
Picture Coordinator: Linda Yates
Photographer's Assistant: Rina M. Ganassa
Kitchen Assistant: Chhomaly Sok

Special Contributors: Mary Jane Blandford and
Paula S. Rothberg (food purchasing), Sarah Brash (text),
Peter Brett (recipe development and styling), Shirley
Corriher (food chemistry), Carol Gvozdich (nutrient
analysis), Nancy Lendved (props), Jane Sigal and
Jeannette Smyth (research), CiCi Williamson and Ann
Steiner (microwave section)

THE COOKS

LISA CHERKASKY has worked as
a chef in Madison, Wisconsin,
and in Washington, D.C., at Le
Pavillon and Le Lion d'Or restau-
rants. She is a graduate of The
Culinary Institute of America at
Hyde Park, New York.

ADAM DE VITO began his cooking apprenticeship at L'Auberge
Chez Francois near Washington,
D.C., when he was only 14. He
has worked at Le Pavillon restaurant, taught with cookbook
author Madeleine Kamman and
conducted classes at L'Académie de Cuisine in Maryland.

JOHN T. SHAFFER is a graduate
of The Culinary Institute of
America. He has had broad ex-
perience as a chef, including five
years at The Four Seasons Hotel
in Washington, D.C., where he
was *chef saucier* at Aux Beaux
Champs restaurant.

THE CONSULTANT

CAROL CUTLER is the prizewinning author of many cookbooks; she also writes about food and entertaining for
national magazines and newspapers. During the 12 years
she lived in France, she studied at the Cordon Bleu and
the École des Trois Gourmandes, as well as with private
chefs. She is a member of the Cercle des Gourmettes,
as well as a charter member and past president of Les
Dames d'Escoffier.

THE NUTRITION CONSULTANT

JANET TENNEY has been involved in nutrition and con-
sumer affairs since she received her master's degree in
human nutrition from Columbia University. She is the
manager for developing and implementing nutritional
programs for a major chain of supermarkets in the Washington, D.C., area.

SPECIAL CONSULTANTS

ROLAND MESNIER, Executive Pastry Chef at the White
House, received his training in France, Germany and Eng-
land. Chef Mesnier has won two dozen gold, silver and
bronze medals for his pastry and sugar work. He teaches
at Maryland's L'Académie de Cuisine.

FRANETTE MCCULLOCH, Roland Mesnier's assistant at
the White House, has studied cooking at the Cordon Bleu
in London and at L'Académie de Cuisine. She runs her
own catering business.

Nutritional analyses for *Fresh Ways with Desserts* were
derived from Practorcare's Nutriplanner System and other current data.

Other Publications:

This volume is one of a series of illustrated cookbooks
that emphasize the preparation of healthful dishes for
today's weight-conscious, nutrition-minded eaters.

Fresh Ways with Desserts

BY

THE EDITORS OF TIME-LIFE BOOKS

TIME-LIFE BOOKS / ALEXANDRIA, VIRGINIA

Contents

Dessert's Eternal Role...........6

The Key to Better Eating....................8

1 Fruit's Artful Simplicity......................11

Orange Slices Macerated
in Red Wine and Port.......................12

Poached Apricots in
Caramel-Orange Sauce 13

Orange-Banana Flowers
with Caramel Sauce 14

Segmenting a Citrus Fruit.................14

Papayas and Cantaloupe in Sweet
Jalapeño Sauce 15

Chilies — A Cautionary Note............15

Fresh Fruit in Ginger Syrup...............17

Fig Flowers with Cassis Sauce 17

Peaches with Mint
and Champagne 18

Grapefruit with Grand Marnier.........19

Peppercorn Pears in
Sabayon Sauce.................................20

Plums with Cream 21

Strawberries with
Lemon-Strawberry Sauce 21

Summer Fruit Salad 22

Apple-Prune Timbales
with Lemon Syrup 23

Black Forest Cherries 24

Pitting a Cherry...............................24

Poached Peaches with Berry Sauce ...25

Rum-Soused Plantains with
Oranges and Kiwi Fruits...................26

Summer Fruit Salad

Blueberry-Peach Crumble.................27

Tropical Fruit Compote with Rum 28

Peeling and Slicing a Pineapple.........28

Preparing a Mango 29

Strawberry Blossoms with Pears
and Red-Wine Sauce 30

Pineapple Gratin 31

Baked Plums with Streusel Topping ...32

Mixed Berry Cobbler 33

Ricotta-Stuffed Pears in
Apricot Sauce 34

Chocolate Leaves 35

Making Chocolate Leaves.................35

Nectarine Cobbler............................36

Pears with Filberts 37

Pear and Cranberry Crisp..................38

Apple Brown Betty with
Cheddar Cheese 39

Raspberries and Figs Brûlées 40

Baked Apples Filled with Grapes 41

Champagne Jelly with Grapes 42

Strawberries and Melon
in Fruit Jelly 43

2 Chilly Delights..............45

*Freezing Sorbets, Sherbets
and Ice Creams*................................46

Blueberry Sorbet 46

Apple Sorbet with
Candied Almonds 47

Lemon Cups 49

Lime Cups 49

Kiwi Sorbet......................................50

Cranberry Sorbet 51

Orange and Passion Fruit Cups.........52

A Zigzag Cut for Fruit Cups..............52

Plum and Red Wine Sorbet
with Raisin Sauce 53

Mint Julep Ice 55

Gewürztraminer Sorbet
with Frosted Grapes..........................55

Gin and Pink Grapefruit Sorbet 56

Strawberry and Champagne
Sorbet 57

Frozen Peach Yogurt.........................59

Frozen Vanilla Yogurt........................59

Frozen Raspberry Yogurt...................59

Frozen Banana Yogurt with
Streusel Crumbs 60

Iced Apple Mousse Cake
with Brandy Snaps 61

Two-Melon Ice with Poppy Seeds
and Port Sauce.................................62

Cappuccino Parfaits 63

Frozen Piña Coladas.........................64

Apple Sorbet with Candied Almonds

Sliced Watermelon Sorbet................65

Frozen Lemon-Meringue Torte 66

Frozen Nectarine and
Plum Terrine 67

Grape Pops......................................68

Mango Ice Cream 69

Spiced Coffee Ice Cream 70

Strawberry Ice Cream.......................71

Peach Ice Cream 72

Rum-Soused Plantains with Oranges and Kiwi Fruits

Frozen Lemon-Meringue Torte

Cherry Puffs

4 Festive Treats to Finish a Meal 99

Apple-Filled Buckwheat Crepes
with Cider Syrup 100
Honey-Glazed Buttermilk Cake 101
Orange-Beet Cake............................102
Cherry Puffs 103
Marbled Angel-Food Cake 104
Chocolate Chiffon Cake with
Raspberry Filling 105
Papaya Porcupines with
Coconut Quills 106
Rhubarb Tartlets Topped
with Meringue 107
Oatmeal-Cocoa Kisses 109
Crisp Oatmeal Cookies 109
Amaretti 110
Brandy Snaps....................................111
Shaping Tulipes...............................112
Rolling "Cigarettes".........................112
Stenciling Leaves 113
Shaped Cookies 113
Fig Bars 114
Bananas and Oranges in
Chocolate Puffs 115
Tangerine Chiffon Cake
with Lemon Glaze 116
Lemon Cornmeal Cake
with Blueberry Sauce 116
Glazed Fruit Tartlets 118
Gingery Peach and
Almond Tartlets 119
Lining Tartlet Molds with Dough 119

Cornmeal Tartlets with Tapioca-
Blueberry Filling 120
Pears with a Spiced Walnut Crust 120
Crepes with Glazed Pears 122
Fruit-and-Nut-Filled Phyllo Roll.........123
Berry-Filled Meringue Baskets...........124
Rolled Cherry-Walnut Cake 124

5 Desserts from the Microwave 127

Bourbon Chocolate Squares 127
Fresh Blueberries with a
Dumpling Topping 128
Chocolate Pudding Cake...................129
Baked Apples Filled with
Cranberries and Golden Raisins 131
Vanilla Custard with Yogurt
and Apricots....................................131
Coffee Soufflé 132
Mocha Pudding 133
Tapioca-Rum Pudding
with Orange 134
Maple Custard with Walnuts 135
Rhubarb Applesauce with
Sugar Toast 136
Rhubarb-Gingerbread
Upside-Down Cake 136

Glossary 138
Index 140
Picture Credits 143
Acknowledgments...........................144

Ginger-Date Ice Cream 73
Cherry Ice Cream 74
Avocado and Grapefruit Bombe
with Candied Zest...........................74
Candied Citrus Zest........................75

3 Light and Creamy Favorites 77

Baked Chocolate Custard 78
Amaretto Flan with Plum Sauce 79
Lemon-Buttermilk Custard with
Candied Lemon Slices........................80
Rice Pudding with
Raspberry Sauce 81
French Cream Cheese
with Blackberries................................82
Maple Mousse with Glazed
Apple Nuggets 83
Banana Flan 84
Raspberry Mousse...........................85
Chilled Lemon Mousse
with Blueberries 85
Layered Bavarian 87
Making Italian Meringue 87
Orange and Buttermilk Parfaits 88
Raspberry Soufflés............................89
Mile-High Pie with Two Sauces 90
Two Methods for Swirling Sauces.........91

Raisin Cheesecake............................92
Homemade Yogurt 92
Blackberry Timbales
with Almond Cream 93
Spiced Pumpkin Mousse
with Lemon Cream 94
Indian Pudding with
Buttermilk Cream 95
Folding Mixtures Together...................95
Orange Chiffon Cheesecake................96
Kugel with Dried Fruit 97

Amaretto Flan with Plum Sauce

Dessert's Eternal Role

No one needs a dessert. A plum tart, a blueberry sorbet, a cheesecake are not likely to appear on any nutritionist's list of essential foods. Indeed, it is easy to obtain all the proteins, carbohydrates, fats and other nutrients required for a healthful diet without ever eating a dessert more complex than a slice of ripe melon. Yet for most people there would be something missing in such a regimen, an unassuaged hunger for the sweet taste, the pleasing aroma, the pretty artifice of a dessert — and the deep, abiding satisfaction it provides.

No other category of food highlights the psychological and esthetic dimensions of eating so clearly as desserts do. The fresh tang of strawberry-lemon sauce with strawberry halves provides its own unique delight, as does the quintessential mildness of a soothing custard. There is a gamut of textures to choose from — crunchy, creamy, dense, airy — in tantalizing combination with an even broader range of flavors. And there is diversity of temperature too — what other food can be served warm, at room temperature, chilled or frozen?

table — especially if you prepare the desserts as directed here and serve them in the portions recommended, which average 200 calories. Indeed, nutritionists acknowledge that refined sugar in modest quantities — no more than 10 percent of one's daily caloric intake — is not harmful to a normal person's health.

The recipes in this book strive to limit sugar, honey and other sweeteners to no more than two tablespoons per serving. (In some instances, such as among the frozen desserts, more sugar is needed to guarantee the proper end result.) Of course, sugar is not the sole caloric ingredient in a dessert. Surprisingly, a teaspoon of sugar contains only 16 calories. Fat, with about 33 calories per teaspoonful, weighs in at double that amount.

The fats in desserts — usually in the form of butter, cream or egg yolks — have traditionally made pie crusts flaky, mousses smooth, custards rich. All are of animal origin, however, and all contain saturated fats, which trigger a rise in the level

Be it pastry or pudding, crisp or smooth, icy or hot, the heart of a dessert's appeal is its sweetness. Experiments with newborn babies suggest that humans have an innate predilection for the sweet. Just a few hours after birth, babies express only mild satisfaction at the taste of water, and a slightly acid solution prompts them to screw up their faces. A sugar solution, however, makes them smile — perhaps for the first time.

Desserts are the prime foods of festivity. What wedding or birthday would be complete without its cake, what Thanksgiving without its pie? Desserts, in short, make us feel good.

Controlling ingredients

The desires that desserts so abundantly fulfill can be accommodated without compromising the goal of healthful eating. The 120 desserts in this volume, which have been created and tested in the Time-Life Books kitchens, are intended to successfully round out a meal. With moderation and balance as a guide in menu planning, you can always find a place for dessert at the

of blood cholesterol, so strongly implicated in heart disease. But as the following recipes demonstrate, fats can be curbed without marring a dessert's appeal. Thus butter, cream and egg yolks appear in many of the recipes, but in moderate amounts — enough, certainly, to lend flavor or texture or both. Butter is generally limited to half a tablespoon per serving; sometimes it is paired with margarine to achieve flakiness in pastry without increasing saturated fat. Cream is by and large restricted to a tablespoon per portion, and a single egg yolk is divided among four servings.

Grand effects can be staged at little cost in fat. A custard can delight with fewer egg yolks than normal when the number of egg whites is increased. A small amount of heavy cream, whipped to twice its original volume, adds a rich look and taste but only 45 calories to the pumpkin-lemon mousse on page 94. In many instances, low-fat, low-calorie ingredients such as yogurt and buttermilk yield desserts that are every bit as delectable as those made with richer ingredients.

A similar stratagem can reduce the sugar in recipes. Even for some cakes, cookies, pastries and frozen desserts, where sugar plays a crucial role, quantities can be cut without compromising taste or texture. The results are still sweet, but never cloyingly so.

Throughout this book, the emphasis is on fresh, natural ingredients bursting with good flavor. There are no artificial sweeteners, no nondairy creamers, no imitation egg yolks. Nor is carob substituted for chocolate; though carob has a somewhat similar flavor and lacks saturated fat, its chalky taste makes it inferior. Unsweetened cocoa powder, produced by extracting fat from chocolate liquor, is used wherever it will not diminish texture and flavor. Oatmeal and nuts, strewn over a dessert as a garnish, provide protein, vitamins, minerals such as iron and phosphorus, and fiber — the carbohydrate that is believed to protect against cardiovascular disease and colon cancer. Whole-grain flours come into play, along with the familiar all-purpose and cake flours.

Flavor, not nutritional content, provides the sole incentive for including sweeteners in a dish. No sugar or syrup contains a significant amount of any nutrient. Honey, in particular, enjoys an undeserved reputation as a good source of minerals and B vitamins. However, all honeys share an attribute that makes them a valued ingredient in cakes, cookies and pastries: They are hygroscopic, meaning they absorb water. A dessert baked with honey loses moisture more slowly and stays fresh longer than one made with another sweetener. On humid days, the honey may actually absorb moisture from the air.

The white sugars — granulated and powdered — have a similar taste but differ in use because of their varying textures. Brown sugars possess an earthy flavor that complements such assertive ingredients as grapefruit, raspberries and figs. Combining the lusciousness of maple syrup with the tartness of sour apples in a mousse (page 83) creates an intriguing balance of opposites.

The magic of fruit

Most of the desserts in this volume derive their special identity from fruit. The first of the book's five sections is given over exclusively to recipes that feature fruit, but you will find fruit as well in the four other sections on frozen desserts, airy and creamy desserts, pastries, and microwave cookery.

Fruit has many qualities to recommend it as a dessert base. It is, to begin with, inherently sweet. Natural sugar accounts for 20 percent of the weight of a banana, and more than 60 percent of the weight of a fresh date. For most fruits, the figure falls in the range of 10 to 15 percent. (One food chemist has speculated that the word "lemon" has come to mean something unexpectedly faulty because it is a mouth-puckering aberration in its class, with a sugar content of only 1 percent.) Despite their sweetness, most fruits are low in calories: Ounce for ounce, they contain only one fifth the calories of sugars and syrups. Using fruits is an ideal way to create desserts that satisfy the calorie limit this book seeks to maintain for individual servings.

Besides sweetness at a modest calorie count, fruits boast other advantages. They are good sources of fiber and, as a group, offer a whole alphabet of vitamins. Potassium and phosphorus are among the minerals that fruits contain, and they are remarkably low in sodium and fat. All of this nutritional bounty is wrapped up in packages of gorgeous colors and sculptured shapes, from the pale green contours of the honeydew melon to the shiny quilted oval of the blackberry.

Many of the recipes in this book call for fresh fruits only. When a frozen substitute will work almost as well, the recipe will say so. Frozen raspberries, blackberries and cranberries all yield excellent purées and sauces. Frozen blueberries can be of good quality, and frozen rhubarb is an excellent alternative to the fresh stalks.

Some 100 varieties of fruit are marketed in the United States. No matter what the season, there should be several types available at their peak of maturity: strawberries in the spring, raspberries, peaches and cherries in the summer, apples in the autumn, and oranges, lemons and grapefruit in the winter. Special pleasure lies in seizing them at their moment of perfect flavor, texture and juiciness.

If you purchase fully ripe fruits, plan to use them within a day or two of their peak, for a decline in quality soon sets in. (This is especially true of berries and grapes.) Most ripe fruits — including tropical ones — should be stored in the refrigerator to retard the shift into overripeness.

When only partially ripened fruit is available, keep it at room temperature, out of direct sunlight. To speed the ripening process, pack the fruit loosely in a brown paper bag, then set the bag in a cool, dry spot and fold it closed. Check the contents of the bag every day and transfer the fruits to the refrigerator as they ripen. Containers made of glass, plastic or stainless steel are best for storage — some metals can impart an unpleasant taste. Wash the fruit or wipe it clean with a damp cloth just before serving or preparing it.

Fruit's finest hours

The trick in selecting perfect fruit is to learn to recognize when it is mature, or at the peak of its developmental cycle. No fruit should be picked before it is mature; if it is, it will fail to undergo the complex chemical process of ripening, in which starches are converted into sugar, and color, texture and flavor evolve. Most fruits will ripen properly if picked at maturity, which allows them to be shipped long distances to market without ill effect. A few, however — notably grapes, raspberries, blackberries, strawberries, blueberries and citrus fruit — must ripen on the mother plant. The best guide to maturity is color: If a fruit is green in whole or in part, it will not, in most cases, taste good. Again, exceptions

The Key to Better Eating

Healthy Home Cooking addresses the concerns of today's weight-conscious, health-minded cooks with recipes that take into account guidelines set by nutritionists. The secret to eating well, of course, has to do with maintaining a balance of foods in the diet. The recipes should therefore be used thoughtfully, in the context of a day's eating. To make the choice easier, this book offers an analysis of the nutrients in each recipe, as at right. Unless otherwise indicated, the analysis is for a single serving of the dessert. The counts given for calories, protein, cholesterol, total fat, saturated fat and sodium are approximate.

Interpreting the chart

The chart below shows the National Research Council's Recommended Dietary Allowances of calories and protein for healthy men, women and children, along with the council's recommendations for the "safe and adequate" maximum intake of sodium. Although the council has not established recommendations for either cholesterol or fat, the chart does include what the National Institutes of Health and the American Heart Association consider the daily maximum amounts of these for healthy members of the general population. The Heart Association, among other concerned groups, has pointed out that Americans derive about 40 percent of their calories from fat; this, it believes, should be cut back to less than 30 percent.

The volumes in the Healthy Home Cooking series do not purport to be diet books, nor do they focus on health foods. Rather, they express a commonsense approach to cooking that uses salt, sugar, cream, butter and oil in moderation while employing other ingredients that also provide flavor and satisfaction. Herbs, spices and aromatic vegetables, as well as fruits, peels, juices, spirits and vinegars, are all used toward this end.

In this volume, a conscious effort has been made to limit the desserts to 200 calories per serving — the average comes to about 175

Calories **178**
Protein **4g.**
Cholesterol **8mg.**
Total fat **4g.**
Saturated fat **1g.**
Sodium **15g.**

— and to restrict, wherever possible, the amount of total fat and saturated fat in the recipes. Occasionally, in the interest of taste, texture or even the successful cooking or freezing of a dessert, the amount of sugar or fat has been increased.

When a dessert recipe exceeds the 200-calorie limit, the cook should give special consideration to the overall nutritional content of the meal that is being planned. It is usually possible to compensate for the dessert's greater calorie count by selecting the meal's other components wisely. In several instances, spirits are listed as optional, but they are not included in the analysis accompanying each recipe. The same is true of optional garnishes. It is up to the cook to judge the effect of these ingredients on the nutritional balance of the meal.

The recipes make few unusual demands.

Naturally they call for fresh ingredients, offering substitutes when these are unavailable. (Only the original ingredient is calculated in the analysis, however.) Most of the ingredients can be found in any well-stocked supermarket. Any that may seem unfamiliar are described in a glossary on pages 138 and 139. To help the cook master new techniques, how-to photographs appear wherever appropriate.

About cooking times

To help the cook plan ahead, Healthy Home Cooking takes time into account in its recipes. While recognizing that everyone cooks at a different speed, and that ovens may differ in their temperatures, the series provides approximate "working" and "total" times for every dessert. Working time denotes the minutes actively spent on preparation; total time includes unattended cooking time, as well as time devoted to freezing or chilling a dessert. Because the recipes emphasize fresh foods, they may take a bit longer to prepare than "quick and easy" dishes that call for packaged products, but the payoff in flavor, and often in nutrition, should compensate for the little extra time involved.

Recommended Dietary Guidelines

		Average Daily Intake		Maximum Daily Intake			
		CALORIES	PROTEIN grams	CHOLESTEROL milligrams	TOTAL FAT grams	SATURATED FAT grams	SODIUM milligrams
Children	7-10	2400	22	240	80	27	1800
Females	11-14	2200	37	220	73	24	2700
	15-18	2100	44	210	70	23	2700
	19-22	2100	44	300	70	23	3300
	23-50	2000	44	300	67	22	3300
	51-75	1800	44	300	60	20	3300
Males	11-14	2700	36	270	90	30	2700
	15-18	2800	56	280	93	31	2700
	19-22	2900	56	300	97	32	3300
	23-50	2700	56	300	90	30	3300
	51-75	2400	56	300	80	27	3300

exist — green bananas, for example, will ripen properly. Some fruits, of course — greengage plums, Kadota figs and certain apples and pears among them — are always green-skinned.

In judging the fitness of fruit, keep the characteristics of each type in mind. Here are some guidelines for selecting fruits:

Apricots. Avoid small, hard specimens — they are probably immature and will never acquire good flavor. Choose those with a lush orange color.

Berries. Choose firm, dry berries with no trace of mold. Blackberries should be shiny and truly black, strawberries an intense, shiny red, raspberries brightly hued. Blueberries should be veiled with a whitish, natural coating of wax called the bloom; because the bloom fades about a week after harvest, it is a sure sign of freshness. Large blueberries are considered by many to be the most flavorful; for other berries, size matters little. If you refrigerate such soft-skinned berries as raspberries for a day or so, store them in a single layer to keep bruises or mold from developing.

Cherries. Large, firm cherries are superior in flavor and texture; of all varieties, Bings are the best. Look for dark, shiny skins.

Citrus fruits. Color and size are not clues to flavor and juiciness. Instead, select fruits that are heavy for their size — an indication of abundant juice. Grapefruits should have thin skin; a pointed stem end suggests thick skin. Navel oranges are easier to peel and segment, but Valencia oranges contain more juice.

Figs. These delicate fruits must be picked ripe, kept under constant refrigeration and used quickly. Reject any that smell sour.

Kiwis. This fuzzy, brown, egg-shaped fruit has bright green flesh, tiny black seeds and a tangy flavor. Buy plump, firm fruit and ripen it at room temperature until it's flesh yields slightly to gentle pressure.

Mangoes. Of the several varieties sold in the United States, the Haden is particularly sweet, fragrant and smooth textured; it has yellow skin with a red patch. Ripen mangoes at room temperature and use them promptly.

Melons. The stem end should be fragrant and yield slightly to gentle pressure. Choose a cantaloupe with yellow under the netting. A ripe honeydew's skin is velvety rather than bald and slick.

Nectarines. Choose firm specimens with high color and allow them to ripen at room temperature for a day or two.

Papayas. These tropical fruits have the shape of a pear and the flavor and texture of a melon. They may be either light green or pale yellow, but they ripen to a golden yellow.

Peaches. Choose fruits for their color — creamy yellow or yellow with a red blush — and a distinctive peachy aroma.

Pears. Look for firm, clear-skinned varieties.

Pineapples. Hawaiian pineapples are sweeter and juicier than their Latin American counterparts. Select firm, unbruised fruit with no soft or moist spots.

Plums. For cooking, choose European plums, which have a purple skin and yellow flesh. The larger, Japanese plums, with red or green skins, are delicious raw but are so juicy that they partially disintegrate when cooked.

The special uses of egg white

Another ubiquitous ingredient in this book is egg white. Unlike the yolk, an egg white is free of fat and cholesterol, and it contains only 16 calories. Egg white is a culinary marvel to boot, accounting for the wonderful lightness of meringues, soufflés and angel-food cakes. When egg white is beaten, its elastic protein inflates in a foamy mass up to eight times its original volume.

Use uncracked eggs that have been refrigerated in their carton. Before you break an egg, especially if you are using it raw, rinse its shell to rid it of bacteria. To separate an egg, some cooks crack it into a hand and let the white run between the fingers into a bowl.

Egg whites can be frozen. In fact, an angel-food cake or a chiffon cake will have a better texture if it is made with defrosted egg whites — provided the eggs were fresh when you froze them.

Beating egg whites is simple, but its success depends upon several factors. Allow the whites to come to room temperature; they will whip up faster than when chilled. Be sure that bowl, beaters and whites contain not a speck of fat or yolk, which inhibit the formation of foam. Do not use a plastic bowl; it is virtually impossible to rid plastic of all traces of fat.

A copper bowl, on the other hand, will produce excellent results: A chemical reaction between the whites and the metal makes it hard to overbeat them and ensures that the whites will rise high when cooked.

If you use a metal other than copper, or a glass or ceramic bowl, beat the egg whites until they are slightly foamy, then add a pinch of cream of tartar per white to guard against overbeating. When the whites reach the desired volume, combine them with the other ingredients *(technique, page 95)*. Do not set beaten egg whites aside for long, lest the foam begin to subside. Be sure to refrigerate desserts containing raw egg whites, and consume them within two days; bacteria can multiply rapidly in them.

The final flourish

Whatever dessert you prepare and whatever the occasion, presenting it attractively makes the eagerly awaited finale of a meal even sweeter. You may want to unmold a bombe onto a platter for all to admire before slicing it into serving portions. Glass dishes show off the radiant colors of fruits, sorbets or sherbets, while small bowls or plates create the pleasant optical illusion that a diner's portion is larger than it is. In serving a well-chosen dessert in the style it deserves, you will have fulfilled its timeless role, bringing the meal to a happy and most satisfying conclusion.

1

Fruit's Artful Simplicity

The natural sweetness and succulence of fruits make them the perfect basis for desserts. It is not an easy task to improve upon something that is — when freshly plucked from tree, bush or vine — beautiful, delicious, refreshing and healthful to boot. Such attributes demand that the cook use the lightest of touches in preparing fruit desserts, lest the essential appeal of the principal ingredient be lessened and the effort turned into an exercise in lily gilding.

The recipes in this section fall into three groups, one of which includes presentations of raw fruits prepared in remarkably uncomplicated ways. For the simplest of these desserts, the fruit requires little more than slicing and arranging, with a syrup poured over the top. Some recipes call for a sauce, often made from another fruit for contrasting color and flavor. Naturally, such dishes require the freshest and ripest of fruits, and the utmost care in preparation to preserve their flavor and color. Some fruits, such as apples, bananas, peaches and pears, contain colorless compounds called phenols that cause the fruit to turn brown when it is peeled or cut. Many of the recipes call for combining the fruit with citrus juice or another acid liquid as soon as it is cut to prevent this unattractive, though harmless, discoloration. Chilling the fruit afterward further guards against the effect.

Fruit should be cut in such a way that the pieces retain some of their contours, and thus their distinctive look. Avoid cutting fruit into tiny dice that can be identified only by the palate — knowing what you are eating by sight as well as by taste heightens the pleasure of the dessert.

A short step removed from the raw-fruit desserts are those that require light poaching in a sweet liquid. Care must be taken to cook the fruit over gentle heat just long enough to soften it, so that the fruit maintains its shape and full flavor. Use a nonreactive pan of stainless steel, glazed earthenware or enamel to avoid discoloration or a metallic flavor. When cooled and allowed to steep in its poaching liquid, the fruit acquires magnified flavor.

The desserts are rounded out by cobblers and crisps, in which the fruit is baked with a topping of dough or crumbs, some of oatmeal. These desserts may be baked in individual serving dishes or in a single large one; in either case, the cookware should be attractive enough to bring to the table.

Orange Slices Macerated in Red Wine and Port

Serves 8
Working time: about 20 minutes
Total time: about 2 hours and 20 minutes
(includes chilling)

Calories **145**
Protein **2g.**
Cholesterol **0mg.**
Total fat **1g.**
Saturated fat **1g.**
Sodium **2mg.**

6 large navel oranges
1 cup Beaujolais or other fruity red wine
¼ cup sugar
1 cinnamon stick
⅛ tsp. ground cardamom or allspice
⅓ cup ruby port
2 tbsp. currants
2 tbsp. toasted sweetened dried coconut

With a vegetable peeler, remove the zest from one of the oranges. Put the zest into a small saucepan with the wine, sugar, cinnamon stick, and cardamom or allspice. Bring the mixture to a boil and cook it over medium-high heat until the liquid is reduced to about ⅔ cup — approximately five minutes. Remove the pan from the heat; stir in the port and currants, and set the sauce aside.

Cut away the skins, removing all the white pith, and slice the oranges into ¼-inch-thick rounds. Arrange the orange rounds on a serving dish and pour the wine sauce over them; remove and discard the cinnamon stick. Refrigerate the dish, covered, for two hours.

Just before serving the oranges, sprinkle the toasted coconut over all.

EDITOR'S NOTE: *To toast the coconut, spread it on a baking sheet and cook it in a preheated 325 ° F. oven, stirring every five minutes, until it has browned — about 15 minutes in all.*

Poached Apricots in Caramel-Orange Sauce

Serves 8
Working time: about 45 minutes
Total time: about 2 hours and 45 minutes
(includes chilling)

Calories **137**
Protein **1g.**
Cholesterol **11mg.**
Total fat **3g.**
Saturated fat **2g.**
Sodium **4mg.**

8 large ripe apricots, or 16 small ripe apricots
1-inch length of vanilla bean
1 cup dry white wine
1 cup sugar
1 orange-zest strip, about 4 inches long and 1 inch wide
fresh mint leaves for garnish
Caramel-orange sauce
½ cup sugar
1 tsp. fresh lemon juice
½ cup fresh orange juice
¼ cup heavy cream

Blanch the apricots in boiling water for 10 seconds, then immediately transfer them to a bowl filled with ice water to arrest their cooking. Peel the apricots as soon as they are cool enough to handle. Cut open the groove in an apricot, then gently pry apart the flesh just enough to remove the pit; ease out the pit. Press the edges of the apricot closed. Repeat the process to pit the remaining apricots.

Slit the piece of vanilla bean lengthwise. In a heavy-bottomed nonreactive saucepan set over medium heat, combine the vanilla bean with 1 cup of water, the wine, the cup of sugar and the orange zest. Bring the mixture to a boil, then reduce the heat, and simmer the syrup for five minutes.

Reduce the heat so that the surface of the syrup barely trembles. Add the apricots and poach them, covered, until they are just tender — three to four minutes. With a slotted spoon, transfer the apricots to a plate; discard the poaching syrup. Cover the apricots and chill them for two hours.

While the apricots are chilling, prepare the sauce. In a small, heavy-bottomed saucepan, combine the ½ cup of sugar with the lemon juice and 3 tablespoons of water. Bring the mixture to a boil and simmer it until it turns a reddish amber — five to eight minutes. Immediately remove the pan from the heat. Standing well back to avoid being splattered, slowly and carefully pour in the orange juice, then the cream. Return the pan to the stove over low heat and simmer the sauce, stirring constantly, until it thickens slightly — about five minutes. Pour the sauce into a small bowl; cover the bowl and refrigerate it.

To serve, spoon the chilled sauce onto individual plates and place the poached apricots in the sauce. Garnish each apricot with a mint leaf.

Orange-Banana Flowers with Caramel Sauce

Serves 6
Working time: about 25 minutes
Total time: about 40 minutes

Calories **261**
Protein **2g.**
Cholesterol **0mg.**
Total fat **1g.**
Saturated fat **0g.**
Sodium **1mg.**

1 cup sugar
6 navel oranges
2 large ripe bananas
½ lemon

In a small, heavy saucepan, combine the sugar with ⅓ cup of water. Bring the mixture to a boil and cook it until it turns a reddish amber. Immediately remove the pan from the heat. Standing well back to avoid being splattered, slowly and carefully pour in ¼ cup of water. Return the pan to the heat and simmer the sauce, stirring constantly, for one minute. Transfer the caramel sauce to the refrigerator to cool.

While the sauce is cooling, peel and segment the oranges as demonstrated below. Peel the bananas and slice them diagonally into pieces about ⅛ inch thick. Squeeze the lemon over the banana slices, then toss the slices to coat them with the lemon juice.

To assemble the dessert, arrange five orange segments in a circle on a plate. Place a banana slice over each of the five points where the segments meet. Arrange three orange segments in a loose circle inside the first circle, and place a banana slice over each of the three points where these segments meet. Top the assembly with two orange segments. Quarter a banana slice and arrange the quarters on top of the last two orange segments. Assemble five more orange-banana flowers the same way.

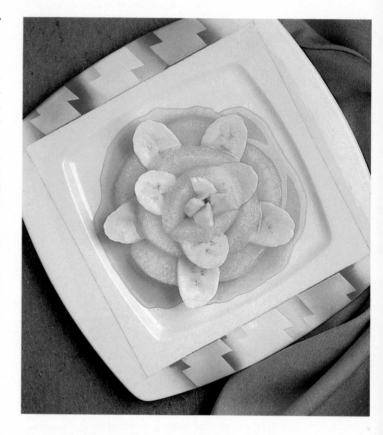

Just before serving the flowers, pour a little caramel sauce around the outside of each one, letting some of the sauce fall onto the petals.

Segmenting a Citrus Fruit

1 TRIMMING THE ENDS. To obtain segments free of pith and membrane from a citrus fruit (here, an orange), use a sharp, stainless steel knife and slice off both ends of the fruit.

2 CUTTING THE PEEL. With the fruit standing on a flat end, slice off the peel in vertical strips, following the contour of the fruit. Rotate the fruit after each cut, and continue to remove strips until peel and pith are completely removed.

3 REMOVING THE SEGMENTS. Working over a bowl to catch the juice, hold the orange in one hand and carefully slice between flesh and membranes to free each segment. Let the segments fall into the bowl as you detach them.

Papayas and Cantaloupe in Sweet Jalapeño Sauce

JALAPEÑO PEPPER ADDS SPARK TO THIS DESSERT.

Serves 8
Working time: about 30 minutes
Total time: about 1 hour and 30 minutes
(includes chilling)

Calories **154**
Protein **1g.**
Cholesterol **0mg.**
Total fat **0g.**
Saturated fat **0g.**
Sodium **8mg.**

1 jalapeño pepper, halved lengthwise and seeded (caution, right)
½ cup fresh lemon juice
1 cup sugar
2 papayas
1 cantaloupe

Preheat the oven to 325° F. Combine the jalapeño pepper, lemon juice, sugar and 1 cup of water in a heavy-bottomed saucepan. Bring the mixture to a boil and cook it until it has reduced to about 1 cup of syrup. Remove the jalapeño pepper and set the syrup aside to cool.

Seed and skin the papayas and the cantaloupe. Cut the papaya into sticks about 1½ inches long and ¼ inch square. Cut the cantaloupe into ½-inch cubes. Mix the fruit with the cooled syrup and chill the mixture for at least one hour before serving.

Chilies — A Cautionary Note

Both dried and fresh hot chilies should be handled with care. Their flesh and seeds contain volatile oils that can make skin tingle and cause eyes to burn. Rubber gloves offer protection — but the cook should still be careful not to touch the face, lips or eyes when working with chilies.

Soaking fresh chilies in cold, salted water for an hour will remove some of their fire. If canned chilies are substituted for fresh ones, they should be rinsed in cold water in order to eliminate as much of the brine used to preserve them as possible.

Fresh Fruit in Ginger Syrup

Serves 6
Working time: about 25 minutes
Total time: about 2 hours (includes chilling)

Calories **149**
Protein **1g.**
Cholesterol **0mg.**
Total fat **0g.**
Saturated fat **0g.**
Sodium **3mg.**

1 tart green apple, quartered, cored and cut into ½-inch pieces
2 ripe peaches or nectarines, halved, pitted and cut into ½-inch pieces
1 pear, peeled, cored and cut into ½-inch pieces
1½ cups blueberries, picked over and stemmed
3 tbsp. fresh lemon juice
2 tbsp. julienned orange zest
2-inch length of ginger root, cut into ¼-inch-thick rounds
⅔ cup sugar

Place the cut fruit and the blueberries in a large bowl. Pour the lemon juice over the fruit and toss well, then refrigerate the bowl.

Pour 4 cups of water into a large, heavy-bottomed saucepan over medium-high heat. Add the orange zest, ginger and sugar, and bring the mixture to a boil. Reduce the heat to medium and simmer the liquid until it is reduced to about 2 cups of syrup. Remove the ginger with a slotted spoon and discard it.

Pour the syrup into a large bowl and let it stand at room temperature for 10 minutes. Add the fruit to the syrup and stir gently to coat the fruit. Refrigerate the dessert, covered, until the fruit is thoroughly chilled — about 1 hour and 30 minutes.

Fig Flowers
with Cassis Sauce

Serves 6
Working time: about 25 minutes
Total time: about 40 minutes

Calories **156**
Protein **1g.**
Cholesterol **0mg.**
Total fat **0g.**
Saturated fat **0g.**
Sodium **5mg.**

2 cups dry white wine
1 tbsp. sugar
¼ cup crème de cassis
12 fresh figs
fresh mint leaves

Combine the wine and sugar in a saucepan over medium-high heat. Cook the liquid until it is reduced to approximately ¾ cup — about 15 minutes. Pour the reduced wine into a bowl and refrigerate it until it is cool — approximately 20 minutes. Stir the crème de cassis into the cooled liquid, then return the sauce to the refrigerator.

With a small, sharp knife, cut a cross in the top of each fig, slicing no more than halfway through. Carefully cut each quarter halfway down into two or three small wedges, leaving the wedges attached at the bottom; each fig will have eight to 12 wedges in all. With your fingers, press the base of the fig to spread the wedges outward like the petals of a flower in bloom. (More cutting may be needed to separate the wedges.)

Set two fig flowers on each of six chilled dessert plates. Drizzle some of the cassis sauce over the flowers, then garnish each serving with a few mint leaves.

Peaches with Mint and Champagne

Serves 4
Working time: about 30 minutes
Total time: about 2 hours and 30 minutes

Calories **134**
Protein **1g.**
Cholesterol **0mg.**
Total fat **0g.**
Saturated fat **0g.**
Sodium **3mg.**

6 ripe peaches
juice of 1 orange
juice of 1 lime
2 tbsp. honey
¼ cup chopped fresh mint
½ cup chilled dry champagne
1 fresh mint sprig for garnish
lime slices for garnish

Blanch the peaches in boiling water for 10 seconds, then drain them and run cold water over them to arrest their cooking. Peel the peaches and halve them lengthwise, discarding the pits. Thinly slice eight of the peach halves lengthwise; transfer the slices to a bowl. Put the four remaining peach halves into a food processor or a blender along with the orange juice, lime juice and honey, and purée the mixture. Blend in the chopped mint, then pour the purée over the peach slices. Cover the bowl and chill it for two hours.

With a slotted spoon, transfer the peaches to a serving platter. Stir the champagne into the purée remaining in the bowl, and spoon the purée over the peaches. Garnish the peaches with the mint sprig and the lime slices just before serving them.

EDITOR'S NOTE: *There is no need to buy a large bottle of champagne for this recipe; small bottles are available.*

Grapefruit
with Grand Marnier

Serves 6
Working time: about 30 minutes
Total time: about 1 hour and 30 minutes

Calories **224**	
Protein **2g.**	2 limes
Cholesterol **0mg.**	2 oranges
Total fat **0g.**	2 lemons
Saturated fat **0g.**	4 grapefruits
Sodium **1mg.**	⅔ cup sugar
	½ cup Grand Marnier or other orange-flavored liqueur

Use a vegetable peeler to remove strips of zest from the limes, oranges, lemons and grapefruits. Cut the strips into julienne. Halve the limes, oranges and lemons, juice them, and strain out the seeds. Pour the juice into a saucepan. Add the julienned citrus zest, the sugar, the liqueur and ⅓ cup of water to the pan; bring the liquid to a boil. Reduce the heat and simmer the mixture until it is syrupy — about 10 minutes.

Peel the grapefruits. Working over a bowl to catch the juice, segment them (technique, page 14). Transfer the segments and their juice to a heatproof bowl. Pour the syrup over the grapefruit and refrigerate the bowl for one hour before serving.

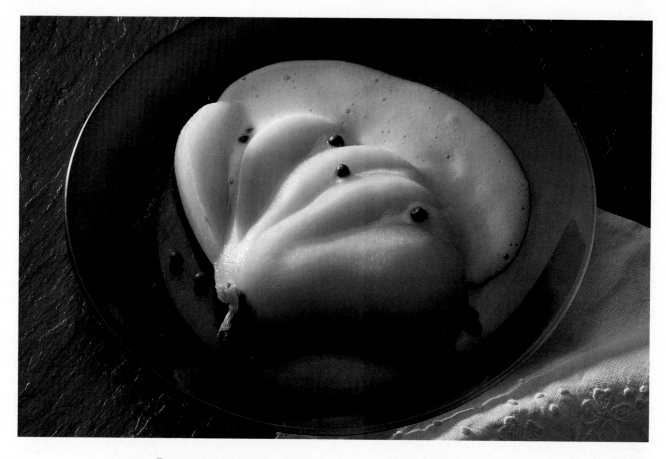

Peppercorn Pears in Sabayon Sauce

Serves 8
Working time: about 1 hour
Total time: about 2 hours

Calories **181**
Protein **2g.**
Cholesterol **69mg.**
Total fat **2g.**
Saturated fat **0g.**
Sodium **19mg.**

1 lemon, halved
4 firm but ripe pears
1 cup sugar
1 cup dry white wine
8 black peppercorns
2 eggs
½ tsp. pure vanilla extract
1 tbsp. vinegar-packed green peppercorns, drained

Prepare acidulated water by squeezing the juice from one of the lemon halves into 1 quart of cold water. Peel, halve, and core the pears, dropping them into the acidulated water to prevent them from discoloring as you work.

In a large, nonreactive skillet, combine the sugar, 1 cup of water, the wine and the black peppercorns. Peel a strip of lemon zest from the reserved lemon half and add it to the skillet. Squeeze the juice of the remaining lemon half into the skillet as well. Bring the liquid to a boil, then reduce the heat to low, and simmer the mixture for five minutes.

Transfer the pears to the sugar syrup and poach them in a single layer for about three minutes on each side. With a slotted spoon, transfer the pears to a plate.

Continue to simmer the poaching liquid over low heat until it is reduced to about 1 cup of heavy syrup — five to 10 minutes. Remove the peppercorns and zest with a spoon. Reserve ⅓ cup of the syrup; pour the remainder over the pears, cover them and refrigerate them until they are chilled — about one hour.

Let the reserved syrup cool for five minutes, then use it to prepare the sabayon sauce. Whisk the eggs in a small, heavy-bottomed saucepan. Pour the syrup into the pan in a thin, steady stream, whisking constantly so that its heat does not curdle the eggs. Cook the mixture over medium heat, stirring constantly until it coats the back of the spoon — three to four minutes. Transfer the custard to a bowl. With an electric mixer set on high, whip the sauce until it has quadrupled in volume and is cool — about five minutes. Blend in the vanilla, then refrigerate the sabayon sauce, covered, until it is chilled — about one hour.

When the pears are chilled, cut them into fans: Set a pear half core side down on the work surface. Holding the knife at a 45-degree angle to the work surface, cut the pear half into five lengthwise slices, leaving the slices attached at the stem end. Gently transfer the pear half to a dessert plate, then spread out the slices in the shape of a fan. Repeat the process to make eight fans in all. Spoon about 1 tablespoon of the chilled sabayon sauce next to each portion. Sprinkle each fan with a few green peppercorns and serve at once.

Plums with Cream

Serves 6
Working time: about 20 minutes
Total time: about 1 hour and 15 minutes
(includes chilling)

Calories **134**
Protein **1g.**
Cholesterol **9mg.**
Total fat **3g.**
Saturated fat **2g.**
Sodium **8mg.**

1½ lb. ripe purple plums, halved and pitted
¼ cup sugar
3 tbsp. arrowroot, mixed with 1 cup water
⅓ cup light cream

Combine the plums, sugar and the arrowroot mixture in a large, heavy-bottomed saucepan. Bring the plum mixture to a simmer over medium heat, stirring constantly. Reduce the heat to maintain a slow simmer and cover the pan. Cook the plums, stirring them from time to time, until they become very soft — about 20 minutes.

Transfer the plums to a food processor or a blender, and purée them. Strain the purée through a sieve into a large bowl. Ladle the purée into six small serving bowls. Cover the bowls and chill them for at least 30 minutes. Spoon 2 tablespoons of the cream over each portion and serve.

Strawberries with Lemon-Strawberry Sauce

Serves 8
Working (and total) time: about 45 minutes

Calories **156**
Protein **2g.**
Cholesterol **69mg.**
Total fat **2g.**
Saturated fat **0g.**
Sodium **19mg.**

2 eggs
¾ cup plus 2 tbsp. sugar
¼ cup cornstarch
grated zest of 2 lemons
½ cup fresh lemon juice
6 cups strawberries, hulled and sliced in half
1 carambola (star fruit), thinly sliced (optional)

In a heavy-bottomed saucepan, whisk together the eggs and the sugar; then mix in the cornstarch, lemon zest, lemon juice and ½ cup of water. Set the lemon mixture over medium heat and stir it continuously until it comes to a boil. Continue cooking and stirring the mixture until it is quite thick — about two minutes more. Set the mixture aside to cool.

Purée 1 cup of the strawberries in a food processor or a blender. Mix the lemon mixture into the purée.

To serve, spoon some of the lemon-strawberry sauce into eight individual bowls or sherbet dishes. Carefully set the remaining strawberries in the sauce; garnish each serving, if you like, with carambola slices.

Summer Fruit Salad

Serves 6
Working time: about 25 minutes
Total time: about 1 hour and 25 minutes

Calories **191**
Protein **4g.**
Cholesterol **2mg.**
Total fat **2g.**
Saturated fat **0g.**
Sodium **35mg.**

1 watermelon (about 6 lb.), cut in half crosswise
juice of 1 lime
juice of 1 orange
¼ cup honey
2 cups blueberries, picked over and stemmed
2 kiwi fruits, each peeled and cut into 8 pieces
1 cup plain low-fat yogurt
2 tbsp. Grand Marnier or other orange-flavored liqueur

With a melon baller, scoop the watermelon flesh from the shell. Set the watermelon balls aside. (If you do not have a melon baller, remove the flesh with a curved grapefruit knife and cut it into uniform cubes, discarding the seeds.) Scrape out and discard any remaining flesh. Notch the rim of one watermelon shell half with a decorative zigzag and refrigerate the shell. Discard the other half.

To make the dressing, combine the lime juice, orange juice and 2 tablespoons of the honey in a large bowl. Add to the dressing the watermelon balls, blueberries and kiwis. Toss the fruit well, then refrigerate the salad for one hour.

To prepare the sauce, whisk together the yogurt, the remaining 2 tablespoons of honey and the liqueur. Refrigerate the sauce.

At serving time, set the watermelon shell on a large platter. Toss the salad once more to coat the fruit with the dressing, then spoon the fruit into the watermelon shell. Serve the chilled sauce in a separate bowl.

Apple-Prune Timbales
with Lemon Syrup

Serves 6
Working time: about 40 minutes
Total time: about 1 hour and 10 minutes

Calories **142**
Protein **1g.**
Cholesterol **5mg.**
Total fat **2g.**
Saturated fat **1g.**
Sodium **2mg.**

1 tbsp. unsalted butter
1¾ lb. tart green apples, peeled, cored and cut into ½-inch pieces
½ tsp. ground coriander
⅛ tsp. ground cloves
2 tbsp. fresh lemon juice
¼ cup brandy
¼ lb. pitted dried prunes, quartered
⅓ cup golden raisins
¼ cup sugar
zest of 1 lemon, finely julienned

Melt the butter in a large, heavy-bottomed skillet over medium-high heat. Add the apple pieces, coriander and cloves, and cook the mixture, stirring constantly, for five minutes.

Stir in the lemon juice, brandy, prunes, raisins, 3 tablespoons of the sugar and ½ cup of water. Cook the compote, stirring frequently, until nearly all the liquid has evaporated — about 10 minutes.

While the apple compote is cooking, combine the zest, the remaining tablespoon of sugar and ¼ cup of water in a small saucepan. Bring the mixture to a boil, then reduce the heat to low; simmer the mixture until the liquid is thick and syrupy — about seven minutes.

Spoon the apple compote into six 4-ounce rame-kins, tamping it down in order to give the timbales a uniform shape when they are unmolded. Let the rame-kins stand at room temperature until tepid — approximately 30 minutes.

Unmold the timbales onto individual plates. Garnish each with some of the lemon zest and drizzle the lem-on syrup over the top.

duced by half — about 15 minutes. (There should be about ¼ cup of thick sauce.) Stir in the kirsch and the vanilla, then pour the sauce over the cherries. Broil the cherries for two or three minutes; serve them hot, with a spoonful of sauce dribbled over each portion.

Black Forest Cherries

Serves 4
Working (and total) time: about 30 minutes

Calories **224**
Protein **2g.**
Cholesterol **21mg.**
Total fat **7g.**
Saturated fat **4g.**
Sodium **73mg.**

1 lb. sweet cherries
¼ cup sugar
1 tbsp. unsweetened cocoa powder
⅛ tsp. salt
¼ cup heavy cream
¼ cup kirsch
½ tsp. pure vanilla extract

Pit the cherries as shown at right.

Combine ¼ cup of water and the sugar in a heavy-bottomed saucepan set over medium-high heat, and bring the mixture to a boil. Add the cherries and stir gently to coat them with the syrup. Cook the cherries for one minute. Using a slotted spoon, transfer the poached cherries to a gratin dish or other heatproof serving dish, and set the dish aside. Remove the syrup from the heat.

Preheat the broiler.

In a bowl, combine the cocoa and salt. Pouring in a steady stream, whisk the cream into the cocoa and salt. Stir the mixture into the syrup in the saucepan. Bring the sauce to a boil, then reduce the heat, and simmer the mixture, stirring occasionally, until it is re-

Pitting a Cherry

1 *INSERTING THE BLADE. Grip a swivel vegetable peeler on either side of the blade, avoiding the cutting edges. Insert the tip into the top of a cherry from which the stem has been removed, and work the peeler's curved tip around the pit.*

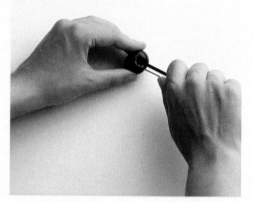

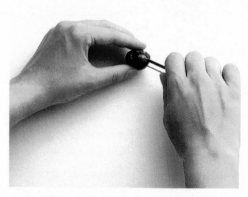

2 *REMOVING THE PIT. Wriggle the tip of the peeler back and forth to loosen the pit from the surrounding flesh. Then pry the pit up through the top of the fruit to dislodge it.*

Poached Peaches with Berry Sauce

Serves 8
Working time: about 30 minutes
Total time: about 2 hours and 30 minutes
(includes chilling)

Calories **122**
Protein **1g.**
Cholesterol **11mg.**
Total fat **3g.**
Saturated fat **2g.**
Sodium **4mg.**

8 firm but ripe freestone peaches
2 cups dry white wine
1 cup sugar
2-inch strip of lemon peel
8 mint sprigs (optional)
Berry sauce
1½ cups fresh or frozen blackberries or raspberries
2 tbsp. sugar
¼ cup heavy cream

Blanch the peaches in boiling water until their skins loosen — 30 seconds to one minute. Remove the peaches and run cold water over them to arrest the cooking. When the peaches are cool enough to handle, peel them and cut them in half lengthwise, discarding the pits.

Put the wine, sugar and lemon peel into a large saucepan. Bring the liquid to a boil, then reduce the heat, and simmer the mixture for five minutes. Add the peach halves to the liquid and poach them until they are just tender — three to five minutes. Using a slotted spoon, transfer the peach halves to a plate. Discard the poaching syrup. Cover the plate and refrigerate it for at least two hours.

To make the berry sauce, purée 1 cup of the berries with the sugar in a food processor or a blender, then strain the purée through a fine sieve into a bowl. Stir the cream into the purée.

To serve, arrange two peach halves on each of eight dessert plates and pour a little of the berry sauce over each portion. Garnish each serving with a few of the remaining berries and, if you like, a sprig of mint.

Rum-Soused Plantains with Oranges and Kiwi Fruits

Serves 6
Working (and total) time: about 45 minutes

Calories **200**
Protein **1g.**
Cholesterol **10mg.**
Total fat **4g.**
Saturated fat **2g.**
Sodium **4mg.**

2 navel oranges
¼ cup sugar
2 tbsp. unsalted butter
2 large ripe plantains, peeled and sliced diagonally into ½-inch-thick pieces
⅓ cup dark rum
2 ripe kiwi fruits
1 tbsp. confectioners' sugar

Squeeze the juice from one of the oranges. Strain the juice into a small bowl and whisk the sugar into it. Set the bowl aside. Peel the second orange; working over another bowl to catch the juice, segment the second orange as shown on page 14. Set the segments aside. Strain the juice in the second bowl into the sweetened juice.

Melt the butter in a large, heavy-bottomed skillet over medium-high heat. Add the plantain slices and cook them for two minutes. Turn the plantains over and cook them on the second side for two minutes.

Pour the orange juice over the plantains and continue cooking them until the liquid reaches a simmer. Cook the plantains at a simmer for two minutes. Pour all but 1 tablespoon of the rum over the plantains. Turn the plantains over and continue cooking them until they are soft — two to four minutes more.

Remove the skillet from the heat; with a slotted spoon, transfer the plantain slices to a flameproof baking dish. Reserve the liquid in the skillet. Arrange the plantain slices in the dish, inserting the orange segments among them.

Peel and chop one of the kiwi fruits, and press it through a sieve into the liquid in the skillet. Stir the sieved fruit into the liquid, then pour the liquid over the plantain slices and orange segments. Peel, quarter, and slice the other kiwi fruit; set the slices aside.

Sprinkle the confectioners' sugar over the contents of the baking dish, set the dish below a preheated broiler just long enough to melt the sugar. Garnish the dish with the kiwi slices. Drizzle the remaining tablespoon of rum over all and serve immediately.

Blueberry-Peach Crumble

Serves 8
Working time: about 30 minutes
Total time: about 1 hour and 15 minutes

Calories **202**
Protein **3g.**
Cholesterol **38mg.**
Total fat **3g.**
Saturated fat **1g.**
Sodium **133mg.**

6 ripe peaches
1 tbsp. fresh lemon juice
¼ cup sugar
3 cups fresh blueberries, picked over and stemmed, or 3 cups frozen whole blueberries

Crumble topping

¾ cup whole-wheat flour
1 tsp. baking powder
¼ tsp. salt
1 tbsp. cold unsalted butter
½ cup plus 1 tbsp. sugar
1 egg
½ tsp. ground cinnamon
1 tbsp. wheat germ

Preheat the oven to 375° F.

Blanch the peaches in boiling water until their skins loosen — 30 seconds to one minute. Peel the peaches and halve them lengthwise, discarding the pits. Cut each peach half into five or six slices. In a bowl, gently toss the slices with the lemon juice and the sugar.

To prepare the crumble topping, put the flour, baking powder, salt, butter and ½ cup of the sugar into a food processor; mix the ingredients just long enough to produce a fine-meal texture. Alternatively, put the dry ingredients into a bowl and cut the butter in using a pastry blender or two knives. Add the egg and blend it in — five to 10 seconds. The topping should have the texture of large crumbs.

Arrange the peach slices in an even layer in a large, shallow baking dish. Scatter the blueberries over the peach slices, then sprinkle the topping over the blueberries. Stir together the cinnamon, wheat germ and the remaining tablespoon of sugar, and strew this mixture over the topping. Bake the dish until the topping is brown and the juices bubble up around the edges — 45 to 55 minutes.

EDITOR'S NOTE: *For added fiber, leave the peach skins on.*

Tropical Fruit Compote with Rum

Serves 8
Working time: about 30 minutes
Total time: about 2 hours and 30 minutes
(includes chilling)

Calories **187**
Protein **1g.**
Cholesterol **0mg.**
Total fat **1g.**
Saturated fat **0g.**
Sodium **2mg.**

½ cup sugar
2 tbsp. fresh lime juice
1 strip of lime zest
1 pineapple, peeled, sliced into 8 rounds and cored (technique, page 28)
2 mangoes, each cut into 8 wedges and peeled (technique, page 29)
3 bananas, peeled, each cut diagonally into 8 pieces
⅓ cup white rum
1 fresh mint sprig (optional)

In a small saucepan, combine ¾ cup of water with the sugar, lime juice and lime zest. Bring the liquid to a boil, then reduce the heat, and simmer the mixture for five minutes. Pour the syrup into a bowl; remove the lime zest and chill the syrup for about two hours.

To serve the compote, arrange the fruit on a serving plate. Stir the rum into the chilled syrup, then pour just enough of the liquid over the fruit to moisten it. If you like, garnish the fruit with a sprig of mint. Serve the remaining syrup in a sauceboat.

Peeling and Slicing a Pineapple

1 *REMOVING THE TOP. With a sharp, stainless steel knife (here, a medium chef's knife), slice off a pineapple's bushy green top. Turn the fruit around and slice off an inch or so from the bottom.*

2 *REMOVING THE RIND. Stand the pineapple on end and slice off a strip of rind, following the contour of the fruit. Cut deep enough to remove most of the dark eyes. Continue slicing until all the rind is removed.*

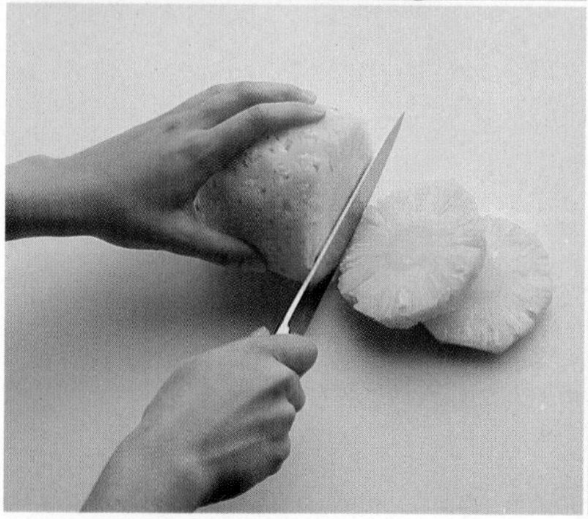

3 *CUTTING SLICES. Cut out any of the eyes that remain. Place the fruit on its side and, steadying it with one hand, divide the pineapple into as many slices as the recipe calls for.*

4 *CORING THE SLICES. With a small biscuit cutter, as shown here, or an apple corer, firmly stamp out and discard the tough, fibrous center of each pineapple slice. If you do not own a small cutter or a corer, remove the center with the tip of a paring knife.*

Preparing a Mango

1 *REMOVING THE PEEL. Cut a thin slice from a mango's stem end. Hold the fruit, stem side up, in the palm of one hand, and use a paring or a utility knife to peel the skin from the flesh, starting each cut from the exposed end.*

2 *CUTTING AWAY THE HALVES. Stand the mango upright on its flat end and slice down one side — following the contour of the large, oval seed — to free one half of the fruit. Cut along the other side of the seed to remove the other half of the mango.*

3 *SLICING UP THE HALVES. Lay a half flat side down on the cutting board. Cut the fruit in half lengthwise, then slice each piece in half again to obtain the wedges called for in the recipe on page 28. (To obtain mango cubes, cut up the wedges and the flesh remaining on the seed.)*

Strawberry Blossoms with Pears and Red-Wine Sauce

Serves 8
Working (and total) time: about 45 minutes

Calories **224**
Protein **1g.**
Cholesterol **4mg.**
Total fat **3g.**
Saturated fat **1g.**
Sodium **5mg.**

2½ cups red wine
⅔ cup sugar
3 lb. firm, ripe pears, peeled, quartered and cored
1 tbsp. unsalted butter
2 tbsp. fresh lemon juice
5 cups hulled strawberries

Combine the wine and ⅓ cup of the sugar in a heavy-bottomed saucepan over medium heat. Cook the wine, stirring occasionally, until it is reduced to about 1 cup — about 30 minutes. Transfer the sauce to a bowl and refrigerate it until it is cool.

While the wine is reducing, cut the pears into thin strips. Melt the butter in a large, heavy-bottomed skillet over medium heat. Add the pears, lemon juice and the remaining ⅓ cup of sugar; cook the mixture, stirring frequently, until almost all the liquid has evaporated — 15 to 20 minutes. Transfer the pear mixture to a plate and refrigerate it until it is cool.

Set eight of the smaller berries aside. Stand the remaining strawberries on a cutting board and cut them into vertical slices about ⅛ inch thick.

Spoon about ¼ cup of the chilled pear mixture into the center of a large dessert plate. Arrange some of the larger strawberry slices in a ring inside the pear mixture, overlapping the slices and propping them at a slight angle to resemble the petals of a flower. Form a smaller ring of strawberry slices inside the first and stand a whole berry in the center. Repeat the process with the remaining pear mixture and strawberries to form eight portions in all.

Just before serving, pour a little of the red-wine sauce around the outside of each blossom, letting a few drops fall onto the petals themselves.

Pineapple Gratin

Serves 6
Working time: about 20 minutes
Total time: about 30 minutes

Calories **170**
Protein **2g.**
Cholesterol **0mg.**
Total fat **1g.**
Saturated fat **0g.**
Sodium **22mg.**

1 large ripe pineapple
2 tbsp. dark raisins
2 tbsp. golden raisins
5 tbsp. pure maple syrup
3 tbsp. bourbon or white rum
1 egg yolk
½ tsp. pure vanilla extract
¼ tsp. ground ginger
1 tbsp. cornstarch
2 egg whites, at room temperature
2 tbsp. dark brown sugar

Preheat the oven to 500° F.

Trim and peel the pineapple as demonstrated in Steps 1 and 2 on page 28. Stand the pineapple upright and cut it in half from top to bottom. Remove the core from each half by cutting a shallow V-shaped groove down the center, then cut each half crosswise into nine slices.

Overlap the pineapple slices in a large, shallow baking dish. Scatter the dark raisins and golden raisins over the pineapple slices. Drizzle 2 tablespoons of the maple syrup over the top, then sprinkle the dish with 2 tablespoons of the bourbon or rum. Cover the dish and set it aside at room temperature.

In a small bowl, blend the egg yolk with the vanilla, ginger, cornstarch, the remaining 3 tablespoons of maple syrup and the remaining tablespoon of bourbon or rum. In a separate bowl, beat the two egg whites until they form soft peaks. Stir half of the beaten egg whites into the yolk mixture to lighten it. Gently fold the yolk mixture into the remaining beaten egg whites.

Bake the dish containing the pineapple until the slices are heated through — about three minutes. Remove the dish from the oven and spread the egg mixture evenly over the fruit. Rub the sugar through a sieve over the top of the egg mixture. Return the dish to the oven and bake the pineapple until the sugar melts and the topping browns and puffs up slightly — about five minutes. Serve the gratin immediately.

Baked Plums
with Streusel Topping

Serves 8
Working time: about 30 minutes
Total time: about 45 minutes

Calories **183**
Protein **2g.**
Cholesterol **8mg.**
Total fat **6g.**
Saturated fat **2g.**
Sodium **5mg.**

8 ripe purple plums, quartered and pitted	
1 cup brandy	
¼ cup dark brown sugar	
grated zest of 1 orange	
Streusel topping	
¼ cup oatmeal	
¼ cup unbleached all-purpose flour	
2 tbsp. unsalted butter, softened	
5 tbsp. dark brown sugar	

¼ cup walnuts, finely chopped
grated zest of 1 orange

Arrange the plum quarters skin side up in an 8-inch-square baking dish. Preheat the oven to 400° F.

Combine the brandy, brown sugar and orange zest in a small saucepan. Bring the mixture to a boil, then cook it until the liquid is reduced to ¼ cup — about five minutes. Pour the brandy syrup evenly over the plums.

To make the streusel topping, chop the oatmeal in a food processor or a blender until it is as fine as flour. Transfer the chopped oatmeal to a large bowl and mix in the flour, butter, brown sugar, walnuts and zest. Dot the surface of the plums with spoonfuls of the topping. Bake the plums until the streusel has browned and the fruit juices are bubbling — 15 to 20 minutes.

Mixed Berry Cobbler

Serves 8
Working (and total) time: about 30 minutes

Calories **179**
Protein **2g.**
Cholesterol **11mg.**
Total fat **6g.**
Saturated fat **3g.**
Sodium **5mg.**

2 cups fresh blueberries, picked over and stemmed, or 2 cups frozen blueberries, thawed
2 cups fresh or frozen red raspberries, thawed
2 cups fresh or frozen black raspberries or blackberries, thawed
¼ cup fresh lemon juice
¼ cup sugar
Oatmeal topping
1 cup rolled oats
¼ cup dark brown sugar
3 tbsp. unsalted butter

Preheat the oven to 350° F.

To prepare the topping, combine the oats and brown sugar in a small bowl. Spread the mixture in a baking pan and bake it until it turns light brown — eight to 10 minutes. Cut the butter into small pieces and scatter them in the pan. Return the pan to the oven until the butter has melted — about one minute.

Stir the oats to coat them with the butter and bake the mixture for five minutes more. Set the oatmeal topping aside to cool. (The topping may be made ahead and stored, tightly covered, for several days.)

Put 1 cup of each of the berries into a 2-quart bowl and set them aside. Combine the lemon juice with the sugar in a saucepan and bring the mixture to a boil. Add the remaining cup of blueberries to the syrup; reduce the heat to low and cook the fruit for three minutes. Add the remaining cup of red raspberries along with the remaining cup of black raspberries or blackberries. Bring the mixture to a simmer and cook it, stirring constantly, for three minutes. Pour the cooked fruit into a sieve set over the bowl of reserved berries; use the back of a wooden spoon to press the fruit through the sieve. Stir gently to coat the whole berries with the sauce.

To serve, spoon the warm fruit mixture into individual ramekins or small bowls. Sprinkle some of the topping over each portion.

EDITOR'S NOTE: *If you prefer not to add the oatmeal topping, the fruit mixture may be served on its own, or it may be spooned over frozen yogurt.*

Ricotta-Stuffed Pears in Apricot Sauce

Serves 4
Working time: about 30 minutes
Total time: about 1 hour and 15 minutes

Calories **309**	
Protein **5g.**	*2 cups dry white wine*
Cholesterol **10mg.**	*½ cup plus 1 tbsp. sugar*
Total fat **4g.**	*4 large, firm but ripe pears*
Saturated fat **2g.**	*½ lemon*
Sodium **45mg.**	*½ cup dried apricots, or ⅓ lb. fresh apricots*
	½ cup part-skim ricotta cheese
	½ oz. semisweet chocolate, finely chopped
	4 chocolate leaves (optional; technique, page 35)

Combine the wine, ½ cup of the sugar and 2 cups of water in a large saucepan over medium heat. Bring the liquid to a simmer.

Meanwhile, peel the pears, leaving their stems attached; as you work, lightly rub the cut lemon half over the pears to keep them from discoloring. Using a melon baller or a small spoon, core the pears from the bottom. Squeeze the lemon half into the saucepan, then add the lemon shell to the liquid.

Carefully lower the pears into the simmering liquid. Poach the pears, turning them after five minutes, until they are somewhat translucent — about 10 minutes in all. While the pears are cooking, prepare the apricots. If you are using fresh apricots, blanch them in boiling water for 30 seconds to one minute to loosen their skins, then run cold water over the apricots to arrest their cooking. Peel and pit the apricots. Whether you are using fresh or dried apricots, coarsely chop them.

Remove the pears from the poaching liquid with a slotted spoon and set them upright on a plate to drain. Refrigerate the pears. Reserve 2 cups of the liquid and discard the rest.

Add all but 2 tablespoons of the chopped apricots to the poaching liquid. Continue simmering the liquid until it is reduced to approximately ¾ cup — about 15 minutes. Purée the apricots and the liquid in a food processor or a blender. Refrigerate the purée.

While the poaching liquid is reducing, mix together the ricotta, the chocolate and the remaining tablespoon of sugar. Finely chop the reserved 2 tablespoons of chopped apricots and stir them in. Put the ricotta mixture into the refrigerator to chill.

To serve, fill each pear with one quarter of the chilled ricotta mixture. Pour some of the apricot purée onto each of four plates; set a stuffed pear in the center and garnish the stem end with a chocolate leaf if you wish.

Chocolate Leaves

Makes 8 leaves
Working time: about 20 minutes
Total time: about 1 hour

Per leaf:
Calories **18**
Protein **0g.**
Cholesterol **0mg.**
Total fat **1g.**
Saturated fat **1g.**
Sodium **0mg.**

---

1 oz. semisweet chocolate, chopped

Carefully wash, rinse and dry 8 rose leaves, and set them aside. Put the chocolate into a ramekin or a custard cup. Fill a saucepan 1 inch deep with water and set the ramekin or custard cup in it; bring the water to a simmer. As soon as the chocolate has melted, use a small, clean paint brush or a feather brush to coat one side of a rose leaf with a generous amount of chocolate as demonstrated at right. Set the painted leaf, chocolate side up, on a plate to cool. Coat the remaining leaves, then put the plate into the freezer until the chocolate hardens — about five minutes.

Remove the chocolate leaves from the freezer. Working rapidly from the stem end, peel back a green leaf to separate it from the chocolate leaf. Return the chocolate leaf to the chilled plate. Repeat the process to separate the remaining leaves. Store the chocolate leaves in the freezer until shortly before use; they melt rapidly if the temperature of the room is warm.

EDITOR'S NOTE: *Leftover chocolate can be stored in an airtight container and reserved for another use.*

Making Chocolate Leaves

1 *APPLYING THE CHOCOLATE. Melt chocolate as directed in the recipe. With a small, clean brush, thickly paint one surface of a clean rose leaf. Set the leaf, chocolate side up, on a chilled tray. Coat all the leaves, then cool them in the freezer at least 5 minutes.*

2 *PEELING THE LEAF. When the chocolate has hardened, remove the tray from the freezer. Working rapidly, gently pull the chocolate and rose leaves apart from stem to tip. Refrigerate the chocolate leaves until you are ready to use them.*

Nectarine Cobbler

Serves 8
Working time: about 30 minutes
Total time: about 1 hour and 20 minutes

Calories **283**
Protein **6g.**
Cholesterol **40mg.**
Total fat **4g.**
Saturated fat **2g.**
Sodium **177mg.**

8 large ripe nectarines
⅓ cup light brown sugar
½ tsp. ground cinnamon
½ tsp. grated nutmeg
1 tbsp. fresh lemon juice
2 tbsp. sugar
Cake topping
1 ½ cups unbleached all-purpose flour
1 ½ tsp. baking powder
¼ tsp. salt
½ cup sugar

1 tbsp. cold unsalted butter
1 egg
¾ cup low-fat milk
1 tsp. pure vanilla extract

Preheat the oven to 375° F. Halve the nectarines lengthwise, discarding the pits. Thinly slice the nectarine halves lengthwise. In a bowl, gently toss the slices with the brown sugar, cinnamon, nutmeg and lemon juice. Transfer the contents of the bowl to a large, shallow baking dish and spread out the nectarine slices in an even layer.

For the cake topping, sift the flour, baking powder, salt and sugar into a bowl. Cut in the butter with a pastry blender or two knives, blending the mixture just long enough to give it a fine-meal texture. In a separate bowl, mix together the egg, milk and vanilla, then pour this mixture into the bowl containing the flour. Using a fork, stir the mixture briskly just until it is well blended — about 30 seconds.

Dot the nectarine slices with evenly spaced spoonfuls of the topping, then smooth the topping so that it covers the fruit. Bake the cobbler for 20 minutes, then sprinkle the 2 tablespoons of sugar over the top. Continue baking the cobbler until the topping is brown, puffed and firm, and the juices bubble up around the edges — 20 to 30 minutes more.

Pears with Filberts

Serves 4
Working time: about 30 minutes
Total time: about 45 minutes

Calories **223**
Protein **2g.**
Cholesterol **8mg.**
Total fat **8g.**
Saturated fat **2g.**
Sodium **5mg.**

¼ cup filberts (about 1 oz.)
¼ cup light brown sugar
1 tbsp. cold unsalted butter
4 large ripe pears
1 lemon half
1 tbsp. fresh lemon juice

Preheat the oven to 375° F.

Spread the nuts in a single layer in a small cake pan or a roasting pan. Toast the nuts in the oven for 10 minutes. Test a nut for doneness by rubbing it in a clean kitchen towel; the skin should come off easily. (If it does not, toast the nuts for two minutes more and repeat the test.) When the nuts are done, wrap them in the towel and rub off their skins. Let the nuts cool to room temperature.

Put the nuts, brown sugar and butter into a food processor or a blender, and process them just until the nuts are coarsely chopped. Set the mixture aside.

Preheat the broiler. Peel the pears, then halve them lengthwise, and core them, rubbing them with the lemon half as you work to prevent discoloration. Arrange the pear halves, cored sides up, in a large, shallow baking dish. Moisten the pears with the lemon juice and sprinkle the filbert mixture over them. Broil the pears until the topping browns and bubbles — about two minutes.

Pear and Cranberry Crisp

Serves 8
Working time: about 30 minutes
Total time: about 1 hour and 10 minutes

Calories **188**
Protein **3g.**
Cholesterol **8mg.**
Total fat **5g.**
Saturated fat **2g.**
Sodium **2mg.**

1 lemon
2 cups fresh or frozen cranberries
¼ cup plus 2 tbsp. sugar
4 pears
Oat topping
1½ cups rolled oats
¼ cup unsweetened apple juice
2 tbsp. unsalted butter, melted

With a vegetable peeler, peel the zest from the lemon. Chop the zest finely and set it aside. Squeeze the lemon, straining and reserving the juice.

Combine the cranberries with ¼ cup of the sugar, the lemon zest and ¼ cup of water in a saucepan over medium-high heat. Bring the mixture to a boil and cook it, stirring occasionally, until the berries burst — about 10 minutes. Set the berry mixture aside.

Peel and core the pears, then coarsely chop them. Transfer the pears to a heavy-bottomed saucepan. Dribble the lemon juice over the pears and bring the mixture to a boil. Reduce the heat to maintain a simmer, then cook the mixture, stirring occasionally, until the pears reach the consistency of thick applesauce — 20 to 30 minutes. Set the pears aside.

Preheat the oven to 400° F.

For the topping, mix together the oats, apple juice and butter. Spread the oat mixture on a baking sheet and bake it, stirring occasionally, until it has browned — 20 to 30 minutes. Remove the topping from the oven and reduce the temperature to 350° F.

Spread about 2 tablespoons of the oat mixture in the bottom of a lightly oiled 1½-quart soufflé dish or casserole. Spread half of the pear mixture in the dish, then top it with half of the cranberry mixture in an even layer. Spread half of the remaining oat topping over the cranberry mixture. Repeat the layering process with the remaining pear, cranberry and oat mixtures to fill the dish. Sprinkle the remaining 2 tablespoons of sugar on top. Bake the crisp until the juices are bubbling hot in the center — 20 to 30 minutes.

Apple Brown Betty
with Cheddar Cheese

Serves 6
Working time: about 30 minutes
Total time: about 1 hour and 15 minutes

Calories **253**
Protein **5g.**
Cholesterol **11mg.**
Total fat **4g.**
Saturated fat **2g.**
Sodium **171mg.**

6 firm whole-wheat bread slices, crusts removed
6 large tart green apples
½ cup plus 1 tbsp. sugar
½ tsp. ground cinnamon
1 tbsp. fresh lemon juice
½ cup unsweetened apple juice
⅓ cup grated sharp Cheddar cheese (about 2 oz.)

Preheat the oven to 300° F. Cut the bread slices into ½-inch cubes and spread them out on a baking sheet.

Bake the bread cubes for 10 minutes, stirring them once to ensure that they cook evenly without browning. Remove the bread cubes from the oven and set them aside. Increase the oven temperature to 375° F.

Peel, quarter and core the apples, then cut the quarters into thin slices. In a bowl, gently toss the slices with ½ cup of the sugar, the cinnamon, lemon juice and apple juice. Spoon half of the apple mixture into a 1½-quart soufflé dish. Cover the apple mixture with half of the toasted bread cubes. Form another layer with the remaining apple mixture and bread cubes. Scatter the cheese over the bread cubes and sprinkle the remaining tablespoon of sugar evenly over the top.

Bake the dish until the juices bubble up around the edges and the top browns — about 45 minutes.

Raspberries and Figs Brûlées

Serves 4
Working (and total) time: about 10 minutes

Calories **116**
Protein **1g.**
Cholesterol **5mg.**
Total fat **3g.**
Saturated fat **2g.**
Sodium **11mg.**

1 cup of fresh or frozen whole raspberries, thawed
2 ripe figs, quartered and thinly sliced lengthwise
¼ cup sour cream
¼ cup light brown sugar

Preheat the broiler. Divide the raspberries evenly among four 4-ounce ramekins. Arrange one quarter of the fig slices in each ramekin, overlapping the slices as necessary to fit them in. Spread 1 tablespoon of the sour cream over the fig slices in each ramekin, then top each layer of sour cream with 1 tablespoon of the brown sugar rubbed through a sieve. Set the ramekins on a baking sheet and broil them until the brown sugar melts and the sour cream bubbles — one to two minutes. Serve immediately.

Baked Apples
Filled with Grapes

Serves 8
Working time: about 50 minutes
Total time: about 1 hour and 40 minutes

Calories **165**
Protein **1g.**
Cholesterol **11mg.**
Total fat **5g.**
Saturated fat **3g.**
Sodium **5mg.**

8 baking apples, cored
3 cups Gewürztraminer or Riesling
2 cups seedless grapes, picked over
½ tsp. ground mace
3 tbsp. unsalted butter

Preheat the oven to 400° F.

With a paring knife, cut a ring of semicircles in the skin at the top of each apple; as the apples bake, the semicircles will "blossom" in a floral pattern. Stand the apples upright in a 2-inch-deep baking dish and pour ½ cup of the wine over them. Put the apples into the oven and bake them for 30 minutes.

While the apples are baking, boil the remaining 2½ cups of wine in a saucepan over medium-high heat until only about 1 cup remains. Stir the grapes and mace into the wine, then reduce the heat, and simmer the mixture for 30 seconds. With a slotted spoon, remove the grapes from their cooking liquid and set them aside; reserve the liquid.

Spoon the grapes into the apples. Cut the butter into eight pieces and dot each apple with one piece of the butter. Pour the reduced wine over all and return the dish to the oven. Bake the apples until they are tender when pierced with the tip of a knife — 15 to 30 minutes more.

To serve, transfer the apples to individual plates. If necessary, use a knife to open up the "flower petals" you carved in the top of the apples.

Champagne Jelly
with Grapes

Serves 6
Working time: about 20 minutes
Total time: about 4 hours (includes chilling)

Calories **183**
Protein **3g.**
Cholesterol **0mg.**
Total fat **0g.**
Saturated fat **0g.**
Sodium **8mg.**

1½ lb. seedless grapes, stemmed and washed
5 tsp. unflavored powdered gelatin (2 envelopes)
¼ cup sugar
2 cups chilled dry Champagne

Divide the grapes among six 6-ounce molds; the grapes should fill each mold no more than three-quarters full. (Alternatively, put all the grapes in a single 6-cup mold.) Refrigerate the molds.

Pour 1 cup of water into the top of a double boiler set over simmering water. Sprinkle in the gelatin and heat the mixture, stirring occasionally, until the gelatin dissolves. Add the sugar and stir to dissolve it too. Remove the gelatin mixture from the heat and pour it into a small bowl.

Set the small bowl in a larger bowl filled with ice. Stir the gelatin mixture until it has cooled to room temperature. Immediately add the Champagne, pouring it against the inside of the bowl to preserve as many bubbles as possible. With a spoon, gently blend the Champagne into the gelatin mixture. Ladle the Champagne-gelatin mixture into the molds; spoon the foam that rises to the top back into the bowl. Repeat the ladling and spooning process until the molds are filled to their brims and all the grapes are covered by the liquid. Freeze the molds for 30 minutes, then chill them for at least three hours.

At serving time, dip the bottom of a mold in hot water for three seconds; run a knife around the inside of the mold to break the suction, then invert a chilled plate on top, and turn both over together. Lift away the mold. (If the dessert does not unmold, hold the mold firmly on the plate and give them a brisk shake.) Repeat the process to unmold the other desserts and serve them immediately.

Strawberries and Melon in Fruit Jelly

Serves 6
Working time: about 30 minutes
Total time: about 2 hours (includes chilling)

Calories **115**
Protein **3g.**
Cholesterol **0mg.**
Total fat **1g.**
Saturated fat **0g.**
Sodium **12mg.**

2½ tsp. unflavored powdered gelatin (1 envelope)
½ cup fresh orange juice
1¼ cups fresh grapefruit juice
¼ cup unsweetened white grape juice
1 tbsp. fresh lime juice
2 tbsp. sugar
1 cantaloupe, halved and seeded
½ cup strawberries
1 kiwi fruit, peeled and thinly sliced crosswise
Strawberry sauce
1 cup strawberries
1 tbsp. sugar
½ tbsp. fresh lime juice

Put 3 tablespoons of water into a small bowl; sprinkle in the gelatin and let it stand until it has absorbed all the water and is transparent — about five minutes. Combine the orange juice, grapefruit juice, grape juice, the tablespoon of lime juice and the 2 tablespoons of sugar in a saucepan; bring the mixture to a boil, then immediately remove the pan from the heat. Add the gelatin mixture to the pan and stir until the gelatin is completely dissolved. Chill the fruit-jelly liquid just until it is syrupy — about 30 minutes — then keep it at room temperature.

With a melon baller, scoop out the cantaloupe flesh. Put three or four melon balls in a single layer into each of six 4-ounce ramekins. Pour enough of the fruit-jelly mixture into each ramekin to barely cover the melon balls. Chill the ramekins until the jelly sets — about 20 minutes. Slice the ½ cup of strawberries in half lengthwise. Arrange some of the strawberry halves, their cut sides facing out and their stem ends up, around the edge of each ramekin. Fill the ramekins with melon balls, then pour in enough of the remaining mixture to cover the fruit. Chill the ramekins until this layer of jelly sets — at least one hour.

For the strawberry sauce, purée the cup of strawberries with the tablespoon of sugar and the ½ tablespoon of lime juice. Cover the sauce and chill it.

When the jelly is set, run the tip of a knife around the inside edge of each ramekin. Invert a chilled dessert plate over a ramekin, then turn them both over together and lift away the ramekin. Repeat the process to unmold the other desserts. Pour some of the strawberry sauce around each portion; garnish the desserts with the kiwi slices and the remaining melon balls.

2

Chilly Delights

Desserts that literally melt in the mouth are universal favorites, and ancient ones as well. Two thousand years ago, potentates everywhere from China to Rome refreshed their palates with frosty mixtures of fruit juice and snow or ice. Such chilly delights persist to this day, along with more elaborate versions containing fruit purée, egg whites, or fillips such as almonds, candied citrus zest and bubbling champagne.

Besides sherbets and sorbets, which consist primarily of fruit juice, sugar and water, the following pages present recipes for frozen mousses, yogurts, parfaits and even ice creams without the cream. The textures of these desserts range from the crunchily crystalline to the satiny smooth, but each one delivers sweetness and refreshment at meal's end with very little fat — and sometimes none at all.

Several freezing techniques are used. Sorbets and sherbets are whisked by hand or blended in a food processor during freezing, so that their ice crystals remain small and air is drawn in. Sorbets, sherbets and ice cream may be prepared in a manually-operated or electric ice-cream maker; the more the mixture is agitated as it freezes, the finer the texture will be. This process, called churn-freezing, also draws air into the mixture and gives it a notable lightness. Because ingredients such as sugar and alcohol can hinder the freezing process if too much is used, do not exceed the amounts specified in the recipes.

Frozen desserts can generally be made a day ahead of serving. Beware, however, of storing them too long. No homemade sorbet, sherbet, mousse or bombe will remain in prime condition for more than a few days at a temperature of 0° F. or lower; some, such as orange sherbet, have evanescent flavors and should be eaten the same day they are prepared. Before freezing highly acid fruit desserts, cover them with plastic wrap — their acid content can eat away at aluminum foil.

If a frozen dessert is too hard, refrigerate it for 20 to 30 minutes before serving time to let it soften slightly for easy slicing or scooping. Present the frozen dessert in well-chilled dishes to minimize melting — and, of course, to heighten the pleasure it offers.

Freezing Sorbets, Sherbets and Ice Creams

Frozen desserts count among everyone's favorites. Three different methods for preparing them are examined below. For efficiency, make sure that the dessert mixture is well chilled before you freeze it.

Hand-whisking method

This basic procedure involves placing the dessert mixture in a freezer, then whisking it from time to time as it firms up to break the ice crystals and aerate the mixture. Before starting, turn your freezer to its coldest setting. Use as large a nonreactive metal bowl as will fit into the freezer, or resort to metal ice-cube trays. (Vessels made of glass, a poor conductor of heat, will retard the freezing process.) Place the bowl containing the dessert in the freezer. When a ring of crystals about half an inch wide has formed around the outside edge of the mixture, usually after an hour or two, whisk the mixture. Return the bowl to the freezer and allow another ring of crystals to form before whisking the mixture again. Repeat the whisking a few more times until the dessert is frozen through. After the final whisking, allow the dessert to freeze an additional 15 minutes, then serve it.

Food-processor method

This fast and easy method utilizes a food processor once the dessert mixture has set. Freeze the mixture in a nonreactive metal bowl; when the dessert has solidified — the center may still be soft — break it into chunks and place them in a food processor. (Return the empty bowl to the freezer; you will need it later.) Process the frozen chunks until the dessert has a smooth consistency; be careful not to overprocess it or it will melt. Return the dessert to the chilled bowl and let it sit in the freezer — a process that cooks call "ripening" — for another 15 minutes until it firms up.

Frozen desserts consisting only of fruit juice and a moderate amount of sugar or those containing alcohol will melt faster than those made with fruit purée, a high amount of sugar, egg white, milk or yogurt. They should be broken into chunks, then processed quickly to break down the crystals without melting. Sorbets and sherbets prepared according to the food-processor method will keep, covered, for several days in the freezer; to restore their consistency, however, they will likely need reprocessing followed by 15 minutes in the freezer.

Churning method

The old-fashioned ice-cream maker that demanded half an hour or more of laborious hand-cranking is quickly being replaced by electric and other convenience models, some containing coolants. In using them, be sure to follow the manufacturer's instructions carefully.

Blueberry Sorbet

Serves 6
Working time: about 10 minutes
Total time: 1 to 3 hours, depending on freezing method

Calories **223**
Protein **1g.**
Cholesterol **0mg.**
Total fat **0g.**
Saturated fat **0g.**
Sodium **7mg.**

4½ cups fresh blueberries, picked over and rinsed, or 4 cups frozen unsweetened blueberries

1¼ cups sugar

1 tbsp. fresh lemon juice

Purée all but ½ cup of the blueberries in a food processor or a blender. If you are using frozen blueberries, purée them all; they do not make a suitable garnish. Strain the purée through a fine sieve into a bowl. Discard any solids remaining in the sieve. Add the sugar and lemon juice to the purée, then stir the mixture until the sugar has dissolved.

Freeze the sorbet, using one of the methods described on page 46. Blueberry sorbet is best when served within 24 hours. Just before serving, garnish the sorbet with the reserved fresh blueberries.

Apple Sorbet
with Candied Almonds

Serves 8
Working time: about 50 minutes
Total time: 1 to 3 hours, depending on freezing method

Calories **249**	
Protein **1g.**	10 tart green apples
Cholesterol **0mg.**	juice of 5 lemons
Total fat **2g.**	1⅔ cups sugar
Saturated fat **0g.**	¼ cup slivered almonds
Sodium **2mg.**	1 tbsp. brown sugar

Cut off and discard the top quarter of one of the apples. Using a melon baller or a spoon, scoop the flesh, core and seeds from the apple, leaving a ¼-inch-thick wall. Reserve the flesh; discard the core and seeds. Sprinkle the inside of the apple and the reserved flesh with some of the lemon juice. Repeat the process with all but two of the remaining apples, then freeze the hollowed apples. Peel, seed and chop the two remaining apples, and add them to the reserved flesh.

Put 2 cups of water, 1 cup of the sugar and about half of the remaining lemon juice in a saucepan. Bring the liquid to a boil, then reduce the heat to medium, and simmer the mixture for three minutes. Add the reserved apple flesh and simmer it until it is tender — three to four minutes. With a slotted spoon, transfer the cooked apple flesh to a food processor or a blender. Discard the poaching liquid. Purée the apple; put 2 cups of the purée into a bowl and allow it to cool. If any purée is left over, reserve it for another use.

Stir the remaining lemon juice and the remaining ⅔ cup of sugar into the apple purée. Freeze the mixture, using one of the methods on page 46.

While the sorbet is freezing, put the slivered almonds in a small, heavy-bottomed skillet over medium heat. Toast the almonds, stirring constantly, until they turn golden brown — about five minutes. Stir in the brown sugar, increase the heat to high, and cook the almonds until they are coated with melted sugar — about one minute more. Set the almonds aside.

When the sorbet is firm, scoop or spoon it into the prepared apple cups, then sprinkle some of the candied almonds over each apple. Keep the apples in the freezer until they are served.

EDITOR'S NOTE: *These sorbets are best when consumed within 24 hours of their preparation.*

Lemon Cups

Serves 8
Working time: about 30 minutes
Total time: 1 to 3 hours, depending on freezing method

Calories **52**
Protein **0g.**
Cholesterol **0mg.**
Total fat **0g.**
Saturated fat **0g.**
Sodium **0mg.**

4 lemons, plus ½ tsp. grated lemon zest
½ cup sugar
16 citrus leaves or fresh mint leaves (optional)

Halve the lemons lengthwise, cutting the rind in a zig-zag pattern *(technique, page 52)*. Remove the pulp and seeds from the halves with a melon baller or a small, sturdy spoon. Transfer the pulp to a sieve set over a bowl, and press down on it with the bottom of a ladle or the back of a wooden spoon to extract all the juice. Discard the pulp and seeds and reserve the juice. Lightly pare the bottom of each lemon shell to stabilize it. Freeze the lemon halves.

Strain ½ cup of the lemon juice into a bowl. (Any excess juice may be reserved for another use.) Whisk 1½ cups of water, the grated zest and the sugar into the strained lemon juice, stirring until the sugar has dissolved. Freeze the sorbet, using one of the methods described on page 46.

When the sorbet is firm, spoon or pipe it into the lemon halves and return them to the freezer. If you like, garnish each lemon cup with two of the citrus or mint leaves before serving.

Lime Cups

Serves 8
Working time: about 30 minutes
Total time: 1 to 3 hours, depending on freezing method

Calories **52**
Protein **0g.**
Cholesterol **0mg.**
Total fat **0g.**
Saturated fat **0g.**
Sodium **0mg.**

8 limes, plus 1 tsp. grated lime zest
2 tbsp. fresh lemon juice
½ cup sugar
1 egg white (optional)
8 citrus leaves or fresh mint leaves (optional)

Cut each lime in half lengthwise. Remove the pulp from the shells with a melon baller or a small spoon. Transfer the pulp to a sieve set over a bowl, and press down on the pulp with the bottom of a ladle or the back of a wooden spoon to extract all the juice. Discard the pulp and seeds, and reserve the juice. Lightly pare the bottom of the shells to stabilize them. Freeze the lime shells.

Strain 6 tablespoons of the lime juice into a bowl. (Any extra juice may be reserved for another use.) Whisk in the lemon juice, 1½ cups of water, the lime ▶

zest, sugar and egg white, and stir until the sugar has dissolved. Freeze the sorbet, using one of the methods described on page 46.

When the sorbet is firm, pipe or spoon it into the lime shells and return them to the freezer. If you like, garnish each lime shell with a citrus or mint leaf.

EDITOR'S NOTE: *The egg white called for here keeps the sorbet from freezing too hard, making it easier to pipe. An egg white may likewise be added to any citrus sorbet in this section.*

Kiwi Sorbet

Serves 4
Working time: about 15 minutes
Total time: 1 to 3 hours, depending on freezing method

Calories **190**
Protein **2g.**
Cholesterol **0mg.**
Total fat **1g.**
Saturated fat **0g.**
Sodium **8mg.**

8 kiwi fruits
2 tbsp. fresh lemon juice
½ cup sugar

Cut a thin slice from both ends of a kiwi fruit. Stand the fruit on a cutting board. Remove the rest of the skin by slicing vertical strips from the sides of the fruit, taking care not to cut off too much of the flesh. Peel the remaining kiwis the same way.

Quarter each kiwi fruit and put the pieces into a food processor or a blender. Process the kiwis just long enough to purée them without cracking their seeds. Add the lemon juice and sugar, and blend them in.

Freeze the mixture, using one of the methods on page 46. Serve the kiwi sorbet in scoops.

Cranberry Sorbet

Serves 8
Working time: about 15 minutes
Total time: 1 to 3 hours, depending on freezing method

Calories **166**
Protein **0g.**
Cholesterol **0mg.**
Total fat **0g.**
Saturated fat **0g.**
Sodium **1mg.**

| ¾ lb. fresh or frozen cranberries (about 3 cups) |
| 1½ cups sugar |
| 2 tbsp. fresh lemon juice |
| 1 kiwi fruit (optional), peeled and thinly sliced |

Put the cranberries into a saucepan with 2½ cups of water. Bring the mixture to a simmer and cook it just until the cranberries pop — about two minutes. Pass the mixture through a sieve, rubbing the cranberries through with the back of a wooden spoon. Stir in the sugar and lemon juice, then freeze the mixture as described on page 46.

Serve the sorbet in scoops; if you like, garnish each portion with the kiwi slices.

Orange and Passion Fruit Cups

Serves 8
Working time: about 30 minutes
Total time: 1 to 3 hours, depending on freezing method

Calories **161**
Protein **1g.**
Cholesterol **0mg.**
Total fat **0g.**
Saturated fat **0g.**
Sodium **4mg.**

8 large oranges (about 4 lb.)	
4 passion fruit	
1 cup sugar	

Halve the oranges crosswise, cutting the rind in a zig-zag pattern as demonstrated below. Remove the pulp and seeds from the halves with a melon baller or a small sturdy spoon. Transfer the pulp to a sieve set over a bowl, and press down on the pulp with the bottom of a ladle or the back of a wooden spoon to extract all the juice. Discard the pulp and seeds. Pour 4 cups of the orange juice into a bowl. With a small spoon, scrape any remaining pulp from eight of the orange halves to form cups. Freeze these cups; discard the remaining orange shells.

Cut the tops off the passion fruit. Scoop out the pulp and seeds and purée them in a food processor or a blender. Strain the purée into the bowl with the orange juice, then whisk in the sugar. Freeze the mixture, using one of the techniques described on page 46.

When the sorbet is firm, scoop or spoon it into the frozen orange cups. Return the cups to the freezer for about 30 minutes before serving them.

EDITOR'S NOTE: *An equally delicious sorbet results when tangerine juice replaces the orange juice. The dish may also be prepared without the passion fruit, in which case 2 tablespoons of fresh lemon juice should be used in their stead.*

A Zigzag Cut for Fruit Cups

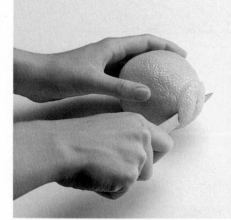

1 *FORMING A FLAT BOTTOM. Holding a citrus fruit (here, an orange) steady, use a small, stainless steel knife to cut a thin slice from its bottom so that the fruit will sit flat when served. (For a lemon, which should be halved lengthwise for greater holding capacity, cut thin slices from two opposite sides to create bases.)*

2 *CUTTING AROUND THE FRUIT. Stand the orange on its flat end. Insert the knife into the midsection at a slant, cutting to the core. Withdraw the knife and make a vertical incision adjacent to the first cut. Alternate slanted and vertical cuts all around the orange until the cuts meet.*

3 *SEPARATING THE TOP AND BOTTOM HALVES. To separate the halves, lift off the top; if the halves stick, twist the top and bottom in opposite directions to separate the pieces. Remove the pulp and juice as indicated in the recipe.*

Plum and Red Wine Sorbet with Raisin Sauce

Serves 10
Working time: about 25 minutes
Total time: about 1 day

Calories **181**
Protein **1g.**
Cholesterol **0mg.**
Total fat **0g.**
Saturated fat **0g.**
Sodium **3mg.**

2½ cups red wine
1¼ cups sugar
1 lb. ripe red plums, quartered and pitted, two of the quarters sliced for garnish
2 tbsp. fresh lemon juice
¼ cup dark raisins
¼ cup golden raisins

Combine 2 cups of the wine with the sugar in a heavy-bottomed saucepan over medium heat. Bring the mixture to a boil, stirring to dissolve the sugar. When the liquid reaches a boil, reduce the heat, cover the pan, and simmer the syrup for two minutes. Stir in the plum quarters; as soon as the syrup returns to a simmer, cover the pan again and cook the plums for four minutes more. Strain ½ cup of the syrup into a small bowl and set it aside for the sauce.

To prepare the sorbet, first purée the plum-wine mixture in a blender or food processor. Blend in the remaining ½ cup of wine and the lemon juice. Let the mixture cool to room temperature, then chill it.

Using one of the methods described on page 46, freeze the sorbet mixture until it is firm but not hard. Transfer the frozen sorbet to a metal mold or bowl. Rap the bottom of the mold or bowl on the counter once or twice to collapse any large air bubbles. Cover the container tightly with plastic wrap and freeze the sorbet overnight.

To prepare the sauce, combine the reserved ½ cup of syrup with the dark and golden raisins in a small, heavy-bottomed saucepan. Quickly bring the mixture to a boil, then immediately remove the pan from the heat. Let the sauce cool to room temperature before refrigerating it; the raisins will plump up.

Shortly before serving time, unmold the sorbet. Dip the bottom of the mold into hot water for 15 seconds; invert a chilled platter on top and turn both over together. If the dessert does not unmold, wrap it in a towel that has been soaked in hot water. After 15 seconds, remove the towel and lift the mold away. Garnish the sorbet with the plum slices, then cut the sorbet into wedges with a cake knife that has been dipped into hot water. Serve some of the raisin sauce with each portion.

Mint Julep Ice

Serves 8
Working time: about 15 minutes
Total time: 1 to 3 hours, depending on freezing method

Calories **180**
Protein **0g.**
Cholesterol **0mg.**
Total fat **0g.**
Saturated fat **0g.**
Sodium **3mg.**

| 1 ¼ cups sugar |
| 1 cup loosely packed fresh mint leaves plus 2 tbsp. chopped fresh mint leaves |
| ¾ cup bourbon |
| juice of 2 lemons |
| 8 mint sprigs for garnish |

In a heavy-bottomed saucepan, combine the sugar, 3 cups of water and the cup of mint. Bring the mixture to a boil over medium heat, stirring to dissolve the sugar. When the mint syrup reaches a boil, cover the pan and boil the syrup for one minute. Pour the syrup through a fine sieve into a medium bowl. Allow the syrup to cool to room temperature and then chill it in the refrigerator for about half an hour.

When the syrup is cold, combine the 2 tablespoons of chopped mint, the bourbon and the lemon juice in a small bowl. Stir the bourbon mixture into the syrup; freeze the mint julep ice until it is firm, using one of the methods described on page 46.

To serve, scoop ½-cup portions of the ice into each of eight sherbet dishes or mint julep cups. Garnish each serving with a sprig of mint.

Gewürztraminer Sorbet with Frosted Grapes

THE WHITE ALSATIAN WINE CALLED FOR IN THIS RECIPE PRODUCES A FULL-FLAVORED SORBET.

Serves 6
Working time: about 10 minutes
Total time: 1 to 3 hours, depending on freezing method

Calories **223**
Protein **1g.**
Cholesterol **0mg.**
Total fat **0g.**
Saturated fat **0g.**
Sodium **11mg.**

| 1 egg white |
| ½ cup seedless green grapes |
| ½ cup seedless red grapes |
| 1 ¼ cups sugar |
| 1 ½ cups Gewürztraminer or Riesling |

Whisk together the egg white and ½ tablespoon of water in a bowl. Add all the grapes and stir to coat them with the egg-white mixture.

Spread the sugar on a dinner plate. Lift a grape from the egg white and roll it in the sugar, coating it with a generous layer of sugar. Transfer the frosted grape to a clean plate. Coat the remaining grapes the same way, transferring each one to the plate as you finish. To solidify the frosting, let the grapes stand at room temperature while you make the sorbet.

Put 2 cups of water and the wine into a bowl, then whisk in the sugar left on the plate. Freeze the sorbet, using one of the methods described on page 46.

Serve the sorbet in scoops, garnishing each portion with a few frosted grapes.

Gin and Pink
Grapefruit Sorbet

Serves 6
Working time: about 15 minutes
Total time: 1 to 3 hours, depending on freezing method

Calories **216**
Protein **1g.**
Cholesterol **0mg.**
Total fat **0g.**
Saturated fat **0g.**
Sodium **2mg.**

4 cups fresh pink-grapefruit juice
1 cup sugar
¼ cup gin
1 tbsp. grenadine (optional)

Combine the grapefruit juice, sugar, gin and grenadine, if you are using it, in a bowl; stir to dissolve the sugar. Freeze the mixture, using one of the methods described on page 46. If you like, present scoops of the sorbet in *tulipes (recipe, page 113)*.

Strawberry and Champagne Sorbet

THE SUCCESS OF THIS RECIPE DEPENDS PARTLY UPON STARTING
OUT WITH CHILLED STRAWBERRIES AND CHAMPAGNE.

Serves 6
Working time: about 15 minutes
Total time: 1 to 2 hours, depending on freezing method

Calories **171**
Protein **0g.**
Cholesterol **0mg.**
Total fat **0g.**
Saturated fat **0g.**
Sodium **4mg.**

2 cups hulled strawberries, quartered and chilled (about ¾ lb.)
¾ cup sugar
2 tbsp. fresh lemon juice
2 cups chilled dry Champagne
6 ripe strawberries for garnish

Put the strawberry quarters, sugar and lemon juice in a food processor or a blender; process the mixture briefly so that the berries are finely chopped — not puréed. Add the Champagne, pouring it slowly against the inside of the bowl to keep it from frothing. Blend quickly to retain as much effervescence as possible, then freeze the mixture using one of the methods described on page 46.

Scoop the sorbet into dessert glasses. If you like, garnish each portion with a strawberry and serve a glass of chilled Champagne alongside.

Frozen Peach Yogurt

Serves 6
Working time: about 15 minutes
Total time: 1 to 3 hours, depending on freezing method

Calories **147**
Protein **5g.**
Cholesterol **3mg.**
Total fat **1g.**
Saturated fat **1g.**
Sodium **58mg.**

1½ lb. ripe peaches
2 tbsp. fresh lemon juice, plus 1 tsp. grated lemon zest
1 tbsp. grated orange zest
1½ cups plain low-fat yogurt
2 egg whites
⅓ cup honey
3 tbsp. cognac or brandy (optional)

Leaving the peaches unpeeled, halve and pit them. Set one of the peach halves aside. Put the remaining peach halves into a food processor or a blender, along with the lemon juice, lemon zest and orange zest; purée the mixture. Add the yogurt, the egg whites, the honey, and the cognac if you are using it, and blend the mixture for five seconds.

Freeze the mixture, following one of the techniques described on page 46.

Before serving, thinly slice the reserved peach half and use the slices to garnish the frozen yogurt.

Frozen Vanilla Yogurt

Serves 4
Working time: about 10 minutes
Total time: 1 to 3 hours, depending on freezing method

Calories **164**
Protein **9g.**
Cholesterol **9mg.**
Total fat **2g.**
Saturated fat **2g.**
Sodium **123mg.**

½ cup low-fat milk
one 2-inch length of vanilla bean, or 1 tsp. pure vanilla extract
2 cups plain low-fat yogurt
2 egg whites
⅓ cup sugar

If you are using the vanilla bean, warm the milk in a saucepan over low heat. Split the vanilla bean lengthwise and add it to the milk. Remove the pan from the heat and let the vanilla bean steep until the milk has cooled to room temperature — about 15 minutes.

Remove the bean from the milk and scrape the seeds inside it into the milk. If you are using vanilla extract, simply combine the unheated milk with the vanilla.

Whisk the yogurt, egg whites and sugar into the milk. Freeze the mixture using one of the methods described on page 46.

Frozen Raspberry Yogurt

Serves 6
Working time: about 15 minutes
Total time: 1 to 3 hours, depending on freezing method

Calories **138**
Protein **5g.**
Cholesterol **5mg.**
Total fat **1g.**
Saturated fat **1g.**
Sodium **70mg.**

2½ cups fresh or whole frozen raspberries, thawed
2 cups plain low-fat yogurt
½ cup sugar
2 egg whites
¼ cup cassis (optional)

Purée the raspberries in a food processor or a blender. Then, to remove the raspberry seeds, pass the purée through a fine sieve into a bowl; use a spatula to force the purée through the wire mesh. Combine the purée with the yogurt and sugar, whisk in the egg whites, then freeze the mixture using one of the methods described on page 46.

Pass the cassis separately so that each diner can pour a little over the yogurt.

EDITOR'S NOTE: *If desired, two yogurts can be swirled together. Make vanilla frozen yogurt (recipe above). Spoon the frozen raspberry yogurt inside a pastry bag, keeping it to one side; spoon the frozen vanilla yogurt on top of the raspberry yogurt, filling the other side of the bag. Pipe out the two yogurts together in a mounting spiral.*

Frozen Banana Yogurt with Streusel Crumbs

Serves 8
Working time: about 15 minutes
Total time: 1 to 3 hours, depending on freezing method

Calories **190**
Protein **6g.**
Cholesterol **8mg.**
Total fat **3g.**
Saturated fat **2g.**
Sodium **101mg.**

2 large bananas (about ¾ lb.)
2 tbsp. fresh lemon juice
2 cups plain low-fat yogurt
2 egg whites, at room temperature
⅓ cup white sugar
3 slices whole-wheat bread
1 tbsp. unsalted butter
¼ cup light brown sugar
1 tbsp. finely chopped walnuts

Purée the bananas and lemon juice in a food processor or a blender. Add the yogurt, egg whites and white sugar, and blend the mixture for five seconds.

Freeze the yogurt mixture, using one of the methods described on page 46.

While the yogurt mixture is freezing, make the streusel: Preheat the oven to 325° F. Tear each slice of bread into three or four pieces; put the bread pieces in a food processor or a blender and process them until they are reduced to fine crumbs. Spread the crumbs in a baking pan and bake them, stirring once or twice to ensure even cooking, until they are crisp — about 15 minutes. Cut the butter into small bits and scatter them over the bread crumbs. Return the pan to the oven just long enough to melt the butter — about one minute. Stir the bread crumbs to coat them with the butter, then transfer the mixture to a bowl. Stir in the brown sugar and walnuts, and set the mixture aside.

When the yogurt mixture is nearly frozen — it will still be soft — stir in all but about 2 tablespoons of the streusel mixture. Return the yogurt to the freezer for approximately 15 minutes more to firm it up. Just before serving the yogurt, sprinkle the reserved streusel over the top.

Iced Apple Mousse Cake with Brandy Snaps

THE RECIPE FOR THE BRANDY SNAPS PICTURED HERE
APPEARS ON PAGE 111.

Serves 12
Working time: about 1 hour
Total time: 2½ to 4 hours, depending
on freezing method

Calories **174**
Protein **2g.**
Cholesterol **10mg.**
Total fat **4g.**
Saturated fat **2g.**
Sodium **29mg.**

2 lb. Golden Delicious apples (about 4 apples)
¼ cup fresh lemon juice
½ tsp. ground cloves
½ tsp. ground cinnamon
2 tbsp. unsalted butter
½ cup sugar
6 egg whites
12 brandy snaps
Apple fans
2 Golden Delicious apples
2 tsp. honey

To make the apple mousse, peel and core the 2 pounds of apples, then cut them into ½-inch chunks. Toss the apples with the lemon juice, cloves and cinnamon.

Melt the butter in a large, heavy-bottomed skillet over medium heat. Add the apple mixture and cook it, stirring frequently, for 10 minutes. Sprinkle in the sugar and continue to cook the mixture, stirring often, for five minutes more.

Put the apple mixture into a food processor or a blender and process it until it is very smooth, stopping at least once to scrape down the sides. Transfer the mixture to a shallow bowl and whisk in the egg whites. Freeze the mixture, using one of the methods described on page 46.

Preheat the oven to 350° F.

To prepare the apple fans, peel the remaining two apples and cut them in half lengthwise. Remove the cores, then slice the apple halves thinly, keeping the slices together. Fan out each sliced apple half on a baking sheet. Drizzle the honey over the apple fans and bake them until they are tender — about 15 minutes. Allow the fans to cool to room temperature, then refrigerate them.

Transfer the apple mixture to a 9-inch springform pan and freeze it until it is solid — about one hour.

To unmold the cake, run a knife around the inside of the pan, then place a hot, damp towel on the bottom for about 10 seconds. Invert a plate on the cake; turn both cake and plate over together. Remove the sides of the pan, and smooth the surface of the cake with a long knife or spatula.

Arrange the chilled apple fans atop the cake; decorate the sides of the cake with brandy snaps.

Two-Melon Ice with Poppy Seeds and Port Sauce

Calories **183**
Protein **2g.**
Cholesterol **0mg.**
Total fat **1g.**
Saturated fat **0g.**
Sodium **22mg.**

Serves 8
Working time: about 15 minutes
Total time: 1 to 3 hours, depending on freezing method

1 ripe honeydew melon (about 5 lb.)
1 ripe cantaloupe (about 3 lb.)
1 tsp. poppy seeds
⅛ tsp. ground mace
¼ cup fresh lemon juice
1 to 1⅓ cups sugar, depending on the sweetness of the melon
Port sauce (optional)
1½ cups ruby port
2 tsp. cornstarch

Port sauce:
Calories **64**
Protein **0g.**
Cholesterol **0mg.**
Total fat **0g.**
Saturated fat **0g.**
Sodium **2mg.**

With a narrow-bladed knife, halve the honeydew melon crosswise, using a zigzag cut to produce a sawtooth pattern in the rind. Remove and discard the seeds. Select the most attractive half of the melon for serving; with a melon baller, scoop from it 1 to 1½ cups of melon balls. Refrigerate the melon balls in a large bowl. Cut enough 1-inch chunks from the flesh of the other melon half to measure 2¾ cups. Purée the chunks in a food processor or a blender — there should be about 2 cups of purée. If the purée measures less than 2 cups, process more melon chunks; if it measures more than 2 cups, reserve the excess for another use. Refrigerate the purée.

Slice the cantaloupe in half with a simple crosswise cut. Scoop out 1 cup of cantaloupe balls and refrigerate them with the honeydew balls until serving time. Cut the remaining cantaloupe into chunks and purée the chunks to produce 2 cups of purée. Stir the cantaloupe and honeydew purées together and chill them.

Discard all the melon shells except the honeydew half you selected for serving. Scrape the inside of the shell clean. Pare a thin slice from the bottom so that the melon will stand upright, then freeze the shell.

Combine the chilled melon purée with the poppy seeds, mace, lemon juice and sugar. Freeze the mixture, using one of the methods described on page 46.

To make the sauce, bring 1¼ cups of the port to a boil in a saucepan. Combine the remaining port with the cornstarch and stir the mixture into the boiling port. Cook the sauce, stirring constantly, until it thickens — about one minute. Allow the sauce to cool to room temperature, then chill it.

Use an ice-cream scoop to fill the frozen honeydew shell with balls of the melon ice. Scatter the chilled melon balls over the top and pass the sauce separately.

Cappuccino Parfaits

Serves 8
Working time: about 35 minutes
Total time: 1 to 3 hours, depending on freezing method

Calories **130**
Protein **1g.**
Cholesterol **11mg.**
Total fat **3g.**
Saturated fat **2g.**
Sodium **16mg.**

zest of 1 orange
2 tbsp. instant espresso coffee
1 cup sugar
¼ cup heavy cream
½ tsp. ground cinnamon
2 egg whites
powdered cocoa

In a heatproof bowl, combine the orange zest, espresso, ¾ cup of the sugar and 2 cups of boiling water. Stir to dissolve the sugar, then let the orange zest steep for 10 minutes. Remove the zest and discard it. Using one of the techniques described on page 46, freeze the espresso mixture.

When the mixture is frozen, divide it among eight glass coffee cups or glasses; freeze the containers.

In a small bowl, whip together the cream and cinnamon until soft peaks form; set the mixture aside. In another bowl, whip the egg whites until they can hold soft peaks when the beater is lifted from the bowl. Continue whipping, gradually adding the remaining ¼ cup of sugar, until the whites are glossy and form stiff peaks. Fold the whipped cream into the egg whites. Fill each of the cups or glasses with some of the egg white-cream mixture. Freeze the parfaits until they are firm — about 30 minutes.

Just before serving the parfaits, dust each one with some of the cocoa.

Frozen Piña Coladas

Serves 8
Working time: about 20 minutes
Total time: about 2 hours and 20 minutes

Calories **126**
Protein **3g.**
Cholesterol **2mg.**
Total fat **2g.**
Saturated fat **1g.**
Sodium **78mg.**

½ cup chopped fresh pineapple
½ cup chopped banana
2 cups buttermilk
½ cup sugar
2 egg whites
¼ cup dark rum
3 tbsp. unsweetened shredded coconut for garnish

Process the pineapple and the banana in a blender or a food processor, stopping once to scrape down the sides with a rubber spatula, until every trace of fiber has disappeared and a smooth purée results — about one minute. (There should be approximately 1 cup of purée.) Blend in the buttermilk, sugar, egg whites and rum. Freeze the mixture using one of the methods described on page 46.

Scoop the sherbet into glasses and keep them in the freezer until serving time.

To toast the coconut, spread it in a baking pan and set it in a preheated 350° F. oven. Toast the coconut, stirring every five minutes, until it is lightly browned — 15 to 20 minutes.

Just before serving the sherbets, sprinkle some of the toasted coconut over each one.

Sliced Watermelon Sorbet

Serves 16
Working time: about 20 minutes
Total time: 4 to 6 hours (includes freezing)

Calories **91**
Protein **1g.**
Cholesterol **0mg.**
Total fat **1g.**
Saturated fat **0g.**
Sodium **3mg.**

1 watermelon (about 8 lb.)
1 cup sugar
2½ tbsp. fresh lemon juice
1 cup fresh blueberries

Halve the watermelon lengthwise. Scoop out all the flesh and put it into a large bowl. Select the more attractive half of the watermelon to use for serving; discard the other half. Cut the watermelon half cross-wise into slices about 1 inch thick. Reassemble the slices so that the watermelon shell appears intact, and freeze it until it is rock-hard and the slices are firmly stuck together. (In order for the slices to cohere, it may be necessary to prop the shell in place during freezing.)

Purée the watermelon flesh in several batches in a blender or food processor, then press it through a sieve to filter out the seeds. Measure the strained fruit; there should be about 7 cups. (If you have more or less fruit, increase or decrease the amount of sugar accordingly by 2 tablespoons per cup of fruit.) Stir the sugar and lemon juice into the strained fruit, then freeze the mixture using one of the methods on page 46. No matter which freezing method you select, do not stir the blueberries into the watermelon sorbet until the end of its freezing period.

When the melon shell is frozen solid, fill it with the blueberry-studded sorbet, smoothing the top so the final result will resemble a freshly cut watermelon half. Freeze the assembly until it is solid throughout — at least two hours.

Present the watermelon intact. Using the precut lines as a guide, cut the watermelon into slices.

Frozen Lemon-Meringue Torte

Serves 8
Working time: about 1 hour and 15 minutes
Total time: 1½ to 4 hours, depending on freezing method

Calories **242**
Protein **4g.**
Cholesterol **0mg.**
Total fat **5g.**
Saturated fat **0g.**
Sodium **28mg.**

8 lemons
1¼ cups sugar
2 egg whites
2 tbsp. unsweetened cocoa powder
Almond meringues
2 egg whites
⅓ cup sugar
½ cup blanched almonds, ground
2 tbsp. confectioners' sugar

Grate the zest from three of the lemons and put it into a blender or a food processor. Working over a bowl to catch the juice, peel and segment one of the lemons as shown on page 14. Squeeze the pulpy core of membranes over the bowl to extract every bit of juice. Repeat the process with the remaining lemons. To remove the seeds, strain the lemon juice into the blender or food processor. Add the lemon segments, the 1¼ cups of sugar, the two egg whites and 2¼ cups of water to the zest and juice, and purée the mixture.

Freeze the lemon mixture following one of the methods described on page 46. While the mixture is freezing, make the almond meringues.

Preheat the oven to 200° F. Line a cookie sheet with parchment paper, or butter the sheet lightly and then dust it with flour.

Whip the two egg whites until they form soft peaks. Beat in the ⅓ cup of sugar a tablespoon at a time; when all the sugar has been incorporated, continue beating the whites until they are glossy and hold stiff peaks. Sprinkle the ground almonds over the whites and fold them in.

Fit a pastry bag with a ½-inch plain tip and spoon the meringue into the bag. Pipe the meringue onto the prepared cookie sheet in strips nearly the length of the sheet; the strips should be about 1 inch wide and 1 inch apart. (If you have no pastry bag, shape the strips with a spoon.) Sprinkle the strips evenly with the confectioners' sugar, then bake them for one hour.

Turn off the oven and let the strips dry, with the oven door ajar, for another hour; if necessary, use a wooden spoon to prop the oven door open. Remove the cookie sheet from the oven and gently loosen the meringues. Break the meringues into bars about 3 inches long; when they have cooled, store them in an airtight container until you are ready to decorate the torte.

When the lemon sorbet is frozen, transfer it to an 8- or 9-inch springform pan. Use a rubber spatula to distribute the sorbet evenly in the pan. Rap the bottom of the pan on the work surface to collapse any large air bubbles, then smooth the top of the sorbet with the spatula. Freeze the torte until it is firm — about one hour.

Remove the sides of the springform pan. Slide a knife or a long metal spatula between the torte and the base of the pan, and transfer the torte to a serving platter. Smooth the sides of the torte with a knife dipped in hot water. Press the meringue bars in place in a random pattern over the top and on the sides of the torte. (The torte can be kept in the freezer with the meringue bars attached.)

Just before serving, dust the torte with the cocoa powder: Put the cocoa into a sieve, then tap the sieve gently as you move it over the torte.

Frozen Nectarine and Plum Terrine

Serves 10
Working time: about 45 minutes
Total time: about 1 day (includes freezing)

Calories **192**
Protein **1g.**
Cholesterol **0mg.**
Total fat **1g.**
Saturated fat **0g.**
Sodium **1mg.**

Nectarine sorbet
1 lb. nectarines, halved and pitted
½ cup fresh orange juice
¼ cup fresh lemon juice
¾ cup sugar
Plum sorbet
1 lb. plums, halved and pitted
¾ cup fresh orange juice
¾ cup sugar
Garnish
1 nectarine, halved, pitted and sliced into thin wedges
2 plums, halved, pitted and sliced into thin wedges

To prepare the nectarine sorbet, purée the nectarines, orange juice, lemon juice and sugar in a food processor or blender. Transfer the purée to a freezer container and freeze it, using one of the methods described on page 46. Prepare the plum sorbet the same way and freeze it as well.

When both sorbets are firm but not hard, line a 6-cup loaf pan with plastic wrap.

Put half of the nectarine sorbet into the lined pan, smoothing it out with a rubber spatula. Top the nectarine sorbet with half of the plum sorbet; smooth its top the same way. Repeat the layering process with the remaining sorbet to make four layers in all. To collapse any air bubbles, tap the bottom of the loaf pan on the work surface. Cover the top of the sorbet with plastic wrap and freeze the terrine overnight.

Remove the plastic wrap from the top. Invert the terrine onto a chilled platter. Unwrap the terrine and cut it into ½-inch-thick slices, dipping the knife into hot water and wiping it off between slices. Garnish the slices with the wedges of nectarine and plum.

Grape Pops

THESE FROZEN CONFECTIONS ARE FORMED
IN A MADELEINE TRAY.

Makes 12
Working time: about 30 minutes
Total time: about 1 hour and 20 minutes

Calories **68**
Protein **0g.**
Cholesterol **0mg.**
Total fat **0g.**
Saturated fat **0g.**
Sodium **2mg.**

1 lb. seedless green grapes
1 lb. seedless black grapes
5 tbsp. sugar

Purée the green grapes in a food processor or a blender. Strain the purée through a fine sieve into a small saucepan. Bring the purée to a simmer over medium-high heat, then stir in 2½ tablespoons of the sugar, and remove the pan from the heat. When the mixture has cooled to room temperature, pour it into a 12-space madeleine tray, filling each space to the brim. Reserve the excess purée. Chill the tray in the freezer until the purée has nearly set — about 30 minutes.

Lay the end of a flat stick in the center of each of the six frozen sorbets in the bottom row of the tray; the sticks should overhang the tray's bottom edge. Return the tray to the freezer.

While the tray is chilling, purée the black grapes and pour the purée into the saucepan. Bring the purée to a simmer over medium-high heat, then stir in the remaining 2½ tablespoons of sugar, and remove the pan from the heat. Strain the mixture into a bowl and set it aside to cool.

When the green-grape mixture has frozen solid, remove the madeleine tray from the freezer; pop out the sorbets in the top row and brush their flat sides with the reserved green-grape mixture. Set one of the painted sorbets atop a sorbet that is still in the tray, and press it in place. Repeat the process to form six pops in all, then return the tray to the freezer for 30 minutes.

When the green-grape pops have frozen solid, remove them from the tray mold and return them to the freezer. Clean the mold and use it to make six black-grape pops, using the same method.

EDITOR'S NOTE: *Flat wooden sticks are sold at variety stores.*

Mango Ice Cream

Serves 8
Working time: about 40 minutes
Total time: 1 to 3 hours, depending on freezing method

Calories **156**
Protein **3g.**
Cholesterol **18mg.**
Total fat **5g.**
Saturated fat **3g.**
Sodium **33mg.**

3 large, ripe mangoes (about 3 lb.), peeled and seeded (technique, page 29)	
1½ cups low-fat milk	
⅓ cup heavy cream	
3 tbsp. sugar	
juice of 1 lime	

Cut enough of the mangoes into small cubes to measure 1½ cups; chill the cubes in the refrigerator.

Purée the remaining mangoes in a blender or a food processor and transfer the purée to a bowl. (There should be about 2 cups of purée.) Add the milk, cream, sugar and lime juice, and stir until the sugar dissolves. Freeze the ice cream, using one of the methods described on page 46.

Scoop the ice cream into serving dishes, then serve each portion with some of the chilled mango cubes.

*The five ice-cream recipes that follow contain no heavy
cream, yet each is a delightfully smooth dessert.*

Spiced Coffee Ice Cream

Serves 8
Working time: about 15 minutes
Total time: 1 to 3 hours, depending on freezing method

Calories **158**	1 ½ cups part-skim ricotta cheese
Protein **6g.**	½ cup plain low-fat yogurt
Cholesterol **15mg.**	⅔ cup sugar
Total fat **5g.**	1 cup freshly brewed triple-strength coffee, chilled
Saturated fat **3g.**	½ tsp. ground cinnamon
Sodium **68mg.**	½ tsp. ground cardamom, or ¼ tsp. grated nutmeg
	½ tsp. pure vanilla extract
	1 oz. semisweet chocolate, grated

Purée the ricotta, yogurt and sugar in a food processor
or a blender, stopping at least once to scrape down the
sides; the goal is a very smooth purée.

Whisk the coffee, cinnamon, cardamom or nutmeg,
vanilla and chocolate into the purée. Freeze the mixture, using one of the techniques described on page
46. If you are using the food-processor method, add
the chocolate after you have processed the mixture.

Strawberry Ice Cream

Serves 8
Working time: about 30 minutes
Total time: 1 to 3 hours, depending on freezing method

Calories **157**
Protein **7g.**
Cholesterol **15mg.**
Total fat **4g.**
Saturated fat **2g.**
Sodium **81mg.**

4 cups hulled ripe strawberries
½ cup sugar
1½ tbsp. fresh lemon juice
2 tbsp. Grand Marnier, or 1 tbsp. grated orange zest
1½ cups part-skim ricotta cheese
½ cup plain low-fat yogurt
2 egg whites

In a food processor or a blender, purée the strawberries with the sugar, lemon juice and the Grand Marnier or orange zest. Transfer the purée to a large bowl and set it aside.

Rinse out the food processor or blender. Add the ricotta cheese and the yogurt and purée them, stopping at least once to scrape down the sides; the goal is a very smooth purée. Whisk the ricotta-yogurt purée and the egg whites into the strawberry purée, then freeze the mixture, using one of the methods described on page 46.

Peach Ice Cream

Serves 8
Working time: about 30 minutes
Total time: about 1 to 3 hours, depending
on freezing method

Calories **193**
Protein **8g.**
Cholesterol **18mg.**
Total fat **5g.**
Saturated fat **3g.**
Sodium **95mg.**

2 lb. ripe peaches
1 ½ tbsp. fresh lemon juice
1 ½ cups part-skim ricotta cheese
½ cup plain low-fat yogurt
2 tbsp. sour cream
½ cup low-fat milk
½ cup light brown sugar
2 egg whites
½ tsp. pure vanilla extract
¼ tsp. almond extract

Bring 2 quarts of water to a boil in a large pot. Add the peaches and blanch them until their skins loosen — 30 seconds to one minute. Remove the peaches with a slotted spoon and set them aside; when they are cool enough to handle, peel them, cut them in half and remove their pits.

Cut enough of the peaches into ½-inch dice to measure 2 cups. Purée the remaining peaches with the lemon juice in a food processor or a blender. Transfer the purée to a large bowl and set it aside.

Put the ricotta, yogurt and sour cream in the food processor or blender; purée the mixture until it has a creamy consistency, stopping at least once to scrape down the sides. Blend in the milk, brown sugar, egg whites, and the vanilla and almond extracts, then whisk the mixture into the peach purée.

Stir the reserved peach dice into the purée and freeze it, using one of the methods described on page 46. If you use the food-processor method of freezing, do not add the peach dice until after you have processed the ice cream.

Ginger-Date Ice Cream

THE CREAMY TEXTURE OF THIS LOW-FAT ICE CREAM
COMES FROM THE PAIRING OF RICOTTA CHEESE AND YOGURT.

Serves 8
Working time: about 25 minutes
Total time: 1 to 3 hours, depending on freezing method

Calories **122**
Protein **6g.**
Cholesterol **12mg.**
Total fat **3g.**
Saturated fat **2g.**
Sodium **77mg.**

1 cup low-fat milk
¼ lb. dried dates, cut into small pieces (about 1 cup)
⅓ cup plain low-fat yogurt
1 cup part-skim ricotta cheese
2 tbsp. sugar
2 egg whites
1 tbsp. finely chopped candied ginger
½ tbsp. fresh lemon juice

Warm the milk in a saucepan over very low heat. Remove the pan from the heat and add all but 2 tablespoons of the dates; steep the dates for 10 minutes.

Purée the date-milk mixture in a food processor or a blender, then transfer the purée to a large bowl.

Purée the yogurt, ricotta cheese and sugar in the food processor or blender, stopping at least once to scrape down the sides; the goal is a very smooth purée. Add the yogurt-ricotta purée to the date-milk purée in the bowl, and whisk the two together. Refrigerate the bowl for 15 minutes.

Blend the egg whites into the refrigerated purée, then freeze the mixture using one of the techniques described on page 46. If you plan to use an ice-cream maker, stir the candied ginger and reserved dates into the mixture before freezing it. If you are using the hand-whisking method, stir in the lemon juice, ginger and reserved dates when the mixture is almost solid. For the food processor method, add the lemon juice during the processing, then blend in the ginger and reserved dates.

Cherry Ice Cream

Serves 8
Working time: about 30 minutes
Total time: 1 to 3 hours, depending on freezing method

Calories **178**
Protein **8g.**
Cholesterol **16mg.**
Total fat **6g.**
Saturated fat **3g.**
Sodium **90mg.**

¾ lb. sweet cherries
½ cup sugar
1 ½ cups part-skim ricotta cheese
½ cup plain low-fat yogurt
½ tsp. almond extract
½ tsp. pure vanilla extract
½ cup low-fat milk
2 tbsp. toasted almonds, crushed
2 egg whites

Pit and quarter the cherries, working over a large bowl to catch any juice *(technique, page 24).* Put the pitted cherries, the sugar and ½ cup of water in a heavy saucepan. Bring the liquid to a boil over medium-high heat, then reduce the heat, and simmer the cherries for 10 minutes.

Remove the cherries from the syrup with a slotted spoon and continue cooking the syrup until it is reduced by one half — about five minutes. Refrigerate the cherries and half of the syrup.

Put the ricotta, yogurt, almond extract and vanilla into a food processor or a blender. Purée the mixture, stopping at least once to scrape down the sides; the goal is a very smooth purée. Stir the cherries and the syrup into the ricotta mixture, then add the milk, almonds and egg whites, and mix well. Freeze the mixture, using one of the techniques described on page 46. If you are using the food processor method, do not add the cherries and almonds until after you have processed the mixture.

Avocado and Grapefruit Bombe with Candied Zest

THIS ELEGANT PRESENTATION OF GRAPEFRUIT SORBET AND AVOCADO ICE MILK MAKES AN ELABORATE BUT PERFECT ENDING TO A SPECIAL MEAL.

Serves 12
Working time: about 1 hour
Total time: 2 to 4 hours, depending on freezing method

Calories **263**
Protein **3g.**
Cholesterol **4mg.**
Total fat **9g.**
Saturated fat **2g.**
Sodium **29mg.**

Grapefruit sorbet
4 large grapefruits
1 ½ cups sugar
Avocado ice milk
2 large ripe avocados
1 cup whole milk
1 cup low-fat milk
½ cup sugar
2 tbsp. finely chopped crystallized ginger

Put a 6-cup round mold into the freezer. Using a vegetable peeler or a paring knife, remove the zest from two of the grapefruits. Cook the zest in a saucepan of boiling water for 10 minutes, then drain it. Julienne half of the zest and candy it *(recipe, page 75)*. Set the candied zest aside. Put the uncandied zest into a food processor or a blender.

Pare the pith from the two zested grapefruits and discard it. Cut away all of the peel from the remaining two grapefruits and discard it too. Working over a bowl to catch the juice, cut between the membranes of the grapefruits to free the segments *(technique, page 14)*. Discard the seeds. Transfer the juice and the segments to the food processor or blender, and purée them with the uncandied zest. Add the sugar and process until it is dissolved. Freeze the grapefruit sorbet, using one of the methods described on page 46.

Remove the mold from the freezer and line it evenly with the sorbet, leaving a large hollow at the center for the avocado mixture. Return the mold to the freezer.

Peel and seed the avocados, and purée their flesh. Blend in the whole milk, low-fat milk and sugar. Freeze the mixture, using one of the methods on page 46. Mix in the ginger halfway through the freezing process.

When the ice milk is frozen, spoon it into the hollow in the grapefruit sorbet. Then freeze the mold for one and a half hours. Before serving, dip the bottom of the mold in hot water, then invert a chilled platter over the top and turn the two over together. Lift the mold away. Garnish the bombe with the candied grapefruit zest, and serve immediately.

Candied Citrus Zest

Makes about ¾ cup
Working time: about 20 minutes
Total time: about 35 minutes

*½ cup julienned citrus zest
(orange, grapefruit, lemon or lime)*

¼ cup sugar

Per tablespoon:
Calories **16**
Protein **0g.**
Cholesterol **0mg.**
Total fat **0g.**
Saturated fat **0g.**
Sodium **0mg.**

Put the citrus zest into a saucepan with 1 cup of water and bring the water to a boil. Cook the zest for 15 minutes, then remove it with a slotted spoon, and spread it on paper towels to drain. Pour the water out of the saucepan. Add the sugar, 2 tablespoons of cold water and the drained zest to the pan. Cook the mixture over high heat, stirring constantly, until the zest is coated with white, crystallized sugar — about 3 minutes. Remove the candied zest from the pan and set it on wax paper to dry.

EDITOR'S NOTE: *Candied zest may be stored in an airtight container at room temperature for up to a week.*

3

Light and Creamy Favorites

Not the least of a dessert's appeal is its texture. The fluffier and creamier the dessert is, the more seductive it is likely to be. But all too often people regard such a dessert as an indulgence, equating its creaminess with richness. In this section, you will find recipes for light and creamy desserts that are delightfully low in calories, yet deliver their full amount of satisfaction — mousses, a layered Bavarian, fruit-filled soufflés, even some ethereal cheesecakes. Complementing them are several sturdier desserts: puddings that invoke childhood memories, but with provocative surprises, such as the rice pudding with raspberry sauce on page 81, or the buttermilk sauce that accompanies the Indian pudding on page 95.

Many of these desserts share an ingredient that entails no fat, no calories and no cost — air. Its presence, in large quantities, may define the very character of a dessert. A soufflé — French for "blown" or "whispered" — is basically a structure of egg whites beaten stiff to entrap a maximum of air. During baking, the air heats and expands to push the dessert mixture to new heights.

Beaten egg whites are folded into many other desserts to lighten them, occasionally along with dissolved gelatin for firmness or a little whipped cream for a velvet texture. Or more elaborately, the whites may be used as the base for an Italian meringue, itself the base of several desserts featured here. In preparing Italian meringue, the whites and hot sugar syrup are beaten simultaneously to make a mixture that is more stable than a meringue made with uncooked sugar. Do not let the sugar syrup hit the whisk or beaters as you add it to the whites; if it does, it may splatter onto the sides of the bowl and stick there — or, worse, it may burn the cook. Where recipes call for whipping cream, make sure that the cream is cold, and that the bowl and beaters are too.

Many of the recipes in this section involve the use of a mold. Unmolding the dessert can be as easy as covering the top of the mold with an inverted plate, then turning the mold over and giving it a gentle shake. If the dessert is unyielding, try briefly dipping the bottom of the mold into warm water, or wrap the mold in a damp, hot towel. Failing this, run the tip of a knife around the edge of the mold to break the vacuum that may be keeping the dessert from sliding free.

Baked Chocolate Custard

Serves 8
Working time: about 30 minutes
Total time: about 2 hours

Calories **108**
Protein **4g.**
Cholesterol **73mg.**
Total fat **3g.**
Saturated fat **1g.**
Sodium **71mg.**

2 eggs
½ cup sugar
2 tbsp. unsweetened cocoa powder
¹⁄₁₆ tsp. salt
2 cups low-fat milk
⅓ cup fresh raspberries (optional)

Preheat the oven to 325° F. Whisk together the eggs, sugar, cocoa powder and salt in a heatproof bowl. Heat the milk in a small saucepan just until it comes to a boil. Whisking continuously, pour the hot milk into the bowl. Thoroughly mix in the milk, then pour the mixture into the saucepan.

Cook the mixture over low heat, stirring constantly with a wooden spoon, until it has thickened enough to lightly coat the back of the spoon. Strain the mixture into eight custard cups. Set the custard cups in a roasting pan or casserole with sides at least ½ inch higher than the cups. Pour enough boiling water into the pan to come halfway up the sides of the cups. Cover the pan with a baking sheet or a piece of aluminum foil, then put it in the oven, and bake the custards until the center of one barely quivers when the cup is shaken — 20 to 30 minutes.

Remove the pan from the oven and uncover it. Leave the custard cups in the water until they cool to room temperature, then refrigerate them for at least 30 minutes. If you like, arrange several fresh raspberries on each custard just before serving them.

Amaretto Flan
with Plum Sauce

Serves 6
Working time: about 30 minutes
Total time: about 1 hour and 30 minutes

Calories **249**
Protein **8g.**
Cholesterol **98mg.**
Total fat **7g.**
Saturated fat **2g.**
Sodium **96mg.**

¼ cup sliced almonds
1 ¼ tsp. ground cinnamon
5 tbsp. sugar
2 eggs, plus 2 egg whites
¼ cup amaretto
¼ cup honey
2 ¼ cups low-fat milk
4 ripe red plums, quartered and pitted
2 tsp. fresh lemon juice

Preheat the oven to 325° F. Spread the almonds in a small baking pan and toast them in the oven as it preheats until they are golden — about 25 minutes.

Lightly butter six 4-ounce ramekins. (If you do not have ramekins, you may use ovenproof custard cups.) In a small dish, mix ¾ teaspoon of the cinnamon with 2 tablespoons of the sugar. Put about 1 teaspoon of the cinnamon-and-sugar mixture into each ramekin, then tilt it in all directions to coat its buttered sides and bottom. Put the ramekins into a large, ovenproof baking dish and refrigerate them.

In a large bowl, whisk together the eggs, egg whites, amaretto, honey and the remaining ½ teaspoon of cinnamon. Whisk in the milk, then pour the flan mixture into the chilled ramekins, filling each to within ¼ inch of the top.

Place the baking dish with the filled ramekins in the preheated oven. Pour enough hot tap water into the baking dish to come two thirds of the way up the sides of the ramekins. Bake the flans until a thin-bladed knife inserted in the center of one comes out clean — about 30 minutes. Remove the ramekins from their water bath and let them stand for half an hour.

While the flans cool, prepare the plum sauce: Combine the plums, the remaining 3 tablespoons of sugar and the lemon juice in a food processor or a blender. Process the plums to a smooth purée, then pass the purée through a fine sieve into a bowl to remove the skins. Refrigerate the sauce until it is chilled — about half an hour.

To unmold the cooled flans, run a small, sharp knife around the inside of each ramekin. Invert a serving plate over the top and turn both over together. Lift away the ramekin; the flan should slip out easily. If it does not, rock the ramekin from side to side to loosen it. Ladle some of the plum sauce around each flan; sprinkle the toasted almonds over the top.

Lemon-Buttermilk Custard with Candied Lemon Slices

Serves 8
Working time: about 20 minutes
Total time: about 2 hours and 40 minutes
(includes chilling)

Calories **185**	
Protein **5g.**	2 eggs
Cholesterol **72mg.**	1 cup sugar
Total fat **2g.**	1/3 cup unbleached all-purpose flour
Saturated fat **1g.**	2 tsp. lemon extract
Sodium **115mg.**	3 cups buttermilk
	3 lemons, thinly sliced, for garnish
	1/2 cup blueberries or raspberries for garnish

Preheat the oven to 300° F.

To prepare the custard, first whisk the eggs in a bowl, then whisk in 2/3 cup of the sugar and the flour; when the custard is smooth, stir in the lemon extract and buttermilk. Pour the custard into eight 1/2-cup custard cups and set them on a baking sheet. Bake the custards until they are puffed up and set, and a knife inserted at the edge comes out clean — 15 to 20 minutes. Let the custards cool slightly, then refrigerate them until they are well chilled — about two hours.

To candy the lemon slices, lightly oil a baking sheet and set it aside. Combine the remaining 1/3 cup of sugar with 1/4 cup of water in a small, heavy-bottomed saucepan. Bring the mixture to a boil, then reduce the heat to low, and cook the syrup, stirring occasionally, until the sugar has dissolved and the syrup is clear — about one and a half minutes. Add the lemon slices to the pan; immediately turn the slices over, coating them well, and cook them for about 30 seconds. Transfer the slices to the oiled baking sheet.

To serve, run a small knife around the inside of each custard cup and invert the custards onto serving plates. Garnish each plate with a few candied lemon slices and a sprinkling of fresh berries.

Rice Pudding with Raspberry Sauce

THIS VARIATION ON AN OLD DESSERT OWES ITS VELVETY
TEXTURE TO THE INCLUSION OF PASTRY CREAM.

Serves 8
Working time: about 50 minutes
Total time: about 3 hours

Calories **224**
Protein **7g.**
Cholesterol **44mg.**
Total fat **3g.**
Saturated fat **2g.**
Sodium **142mg.**

4 cups low-fat milk
½ cup long-grain rice
½ cup plus 2 tbsp. sugar
¼ tsp. salt
1 egg yolk
3 tbsp. unbleached all-purpose flour
½ tsp. grated nutmeg
1 tsp. pure vanilla extract
¼ tsp. almond extract
¼ cup golden raisins
2 cups fresh or frozen whole raspberries, thawed
fresh mint leaves (optional)

Bring 3 cups of the milk to a boil in a heavy-bottomed saucepan over medium heat. Reduce the heat to low and add the rice, ¼ cup of the sugar and the salt. Cook the mixture, stirring frequently, for 50 minutes.

To prepare the pastry cream, whisk together the egg yolk and ¼ cup of the remaining milk. Whisk in the flour and ¼ cup of the remaining sugar; then blend in the remaining ¾ cup of milk. Bring the mixture to a boil over medium heat, stirring constantly, then cook it, still stirring vigorously, for two minutes more. Remove the pan from the heat and stir in the nutmeg, vanilla and almond extract.

When the rice has finished cooking, stir in the raisins, then fold in the pastry cream. Transfer the pudding to a clean bowl. To prevent a skin from forming on its surface, press a sheet of plastic wrap directly onto the pudding. Refrigerate the pudding until it is cold — about two hours.

To prepare the sauce, purée the raspberries and the remaining 2 tablespoons of sugar in a blender or a food processor. Rub the purée through a fine sieve with a plastic spatula or the back of a wooden spoon; discard the seeds.

To serve, divide the sauce among eight serving dishes. Top the sauce with individual scoops of pudding; if you like, sprinkle the scoops with some additional nutmeg and garnish each with a sprig of mint.

French Cream Cheese
with Blackberries

THIS DESSERT, WHICH CONTAINS GOAT CHEESE, GOES
PARTICULARLY WELL WITH TART, FRESH FRUIT.

Serves 10
Working time: about 20 minutes
Total time: about 6 hours (includes chilling)

Calories **122**
Protein **12g.**
Cholesterol **6mg.**
Total fat **2g.**
Saturated fat **1g.**
Sodium **345mg.**

1½ lb. low-fat cottage cheese
6 oz. mild, creamy goat cheese
¼ cup sugar
4 cups of blackberries or strawberries

Purée the cottage cheese in a food processor or a blender until it is completely smooth. With the motor running, blend in the goat cheese a tablespoon at a time. Stop once or twice during the process to scrape down the sides. Add the sugar and blend it in.

Cut a single thickness of cheesecloth large enough to encase the cheese mixture as it drains. Wet the cheesecloth in cold water, then wring it out. Line a large sieve, colander, or *coeur à la crème* mold with the cheesecloth, pressing it in place and smoothing it out

with your fingers so that the surface of the finished cheese will be uniformly even.

Spoon the cheese mixture into the lined container. Smooth the top of the cheese mixture and fold the edges of the cheesecloth over it. If you are using a sieve or colander, suspend it over a deep bowl; if you are using a *coeur à la crème* mold, put it on a plate. Refrigerate the assembly until the whey has thoroughly drained from the cheese — about six hours.

To unmold the cream cheese, open the cheesecloth and invert a serving plate over the sieve. Turn both sieve and plate over together, then lift away the sieve and the cheesecloth.

Serve the cream cheese chilled. Ring the plate with some of the berries; present the rest in a separate dish.

Maple Mousse with Glazed Apple Nuggets

Serves 6
Working time: about 1 hour
Total time: about 1 hour and 45 minutes

Calories **216**
Protein **2g.**
Cholesterol **24mg.**
Total fat **7g.**
Saturated fat **4g.**
Sodium **37mg.**

1 tbsp. unsalted butter
2 tart green apples, peeled, cored and cut into ½-inch cubes
1 tsp. fresh lemon juice
½ cup plus 1 tbsp. maple syrup
⅓ cup heavy cream
½ tsp. pure vanilla extract
3 egg whites, at room temperature
5 tbsp. light brown sugar

Melt the butter in a large, heavy-bottomed skillet set over medium-high heat. When the butter is hot, add the apple cubes and lemon juice; sauté the cubes, turning them frequently, until they are light brown — about 10 minutes. Drizzle 1 tablespoon of the maple syrup over the apple cubes and sauté them for one minute more. Transfer the glazed apple cubes to a plate and refrigerate them.

In a small bowl, whip the cream until it holds stiff peaks, stir in the vanilla, then refrigerate the cream. Put the egg whites into a deep bowl and set them aside.

To prepare the maple flavoring for the mousse, combine ¼ cup of the remaining maple syrup and the sugar in a small, heavy-bottomed saucepan. Bring the mixture to a boil and cook it to the soft ball stage over medium heat *(technique, page 87)*. Begin testing after four minutes: With a small spoon, drop a bit of the syrup into a bowl filled with ice water. When the mixture can be rolled into a ball, start beating the egg whites with an electric mixer on medium-high speed. Pour the hot syrup into the whites in a thin, steady stream, beating as you pour. Continue to beat the whites until the meringue has cooled to room tem-

perature — about seven minutes. Gently fold the whipped cream and the chilled apple pieces into the meringue. (Do not overfold.) Immediately spoon the mousse into six individual cups and refrigerate them for at least 45 minutes.

To prepare the maple sugar, bring the remaining ¼ cup of syrup to a boil in a small, heavy-bottomed saucepan. Reduce the heat to medium and cook the syrup, stirring frequently, until the mixture crystallizes — about 15 minutes. Remove the saucepan from the heat and allow the mixture to cool for 10 minutes, stirring occasionally. Scrape the crystallized sugar out of the pan onto a clean work surface. Using a rolling pin or the bottom of a heavy pan, crush the sugar until it is finely crumbled.

Just before serving, sprinkle some of the maple sugar onto each portion of mousse.

Banana Flan

Serves 8
Working time: about 45 minutes
Total time: about 3 hours and 15 minutes

Calories **158**
Protein **3g.**
Cholesterol **71mg.**
Total fat **2g.**
Saturated fat **1g.**
Sodium **36mg.**

½ cup plus ⅓ cup sugar
4 tsp. fresh lemon juice
1 cup low-fat milk
2 eggs
1 tbsp. dark rum
1 tsp. pure vanilla extract
¼ tsp. ground cardamom or cinnamon
1 cup banana purée (from 2 or 3 bananas)
2 bananas, peeled and diagonally sliced (optional)

Preheat the oven to 325° F.

Begin by caramelizing a 1-quart soufflé dish or a 6-inch-diameter cake pan: In a small heavy-bottomed saucepan, combine ½ cup of the sugar, 1 teaspoon of the lemon juice and 3 tablespoons of water. Cook the mixture over medium-high heat until the syrup caramelizes — it will have a rich brown hue. Immediately remove the saucepan from the heat. Working quickly, pour the caramel into the soufflé dish or cake pan. Using potholders to protect your hands, tilt the dish in all directions to coat the bottom and about one inch of the adjacent sides. Continue tilting the dish until the

caramel has hardened, then set the dish aside.

To prepare the custard, put the milk into a heavy-bottomed saucepan over medium heat. As soon as the milk reaches a boil, remove the pan from the heat and set it aside. In a bowl, whisk together the eggs and the remaining ⅓ cup of sugar, then stir in the rum, vanilla, cardamom or cinnamon, banana purée, and the remaining 3 teaspoons of lemon juice. Stirring constantly to avoid curdling the eggs, pour the hot milk into the banana mixture. Transfer the custard to the caramelized dish.

Set the custard dish in a small roasting pan and pour enough hot tap water into the pan to come 1 inch up the sides of the custard dish. Bake the flan until a knife inserted in the center comes out clean — 20 to 30 minutes. (Take care not to insert the knife so deep that it pierces the caramel coating.) Remove the flan from the hot-water bath and let it cool to room temperature. Put the flan into the refrigerator until it is chilled — about two hours.

To unmold the chilled flan, invert a serving plate over the top of the dish, then turn both over together. The dish should lift away easily; if it does not, turn the dish right side up again and run a small, sharp knife around the top of the custard to loosen it. If you like, garnish the flan with a ring of banana slices. Cut the flan into wedges and spoon some of the caramel sauce over each one before serving.

Raspberry Mousse

Serves 8
Working time: about 20 minutes
Total time: about 1 hour

Calories **149**
Protein **4g.**
Cholesterol **23mg.**
Total fat **6g.**
Saturated fat **4g.**
Sodium **40mg.**

2½ tsp. unflavored powdered gelatin (1 envelope)
½ cup sugar
3 cups fresh or frozen whole raspberries, thawed
1 cup plain low-fat yogurt
½ cup heavy cream
2 egg whites

Sprinkle the gelatin onto ¼ cup of water and let the gelatin soften while you prepare the raspberries. Set 24 berries aside to use as garnish. Pour ¼ cup of water into a saucepan; stir in the sugar and the remaining raspberries. Over medium heat, simmer the mixture for four minutes. Add the softened gelatin and stir until it dissolves — about 30 seconds.

Transfer the raspberry mixture to a blender or a food processor and purée it. Strain the purée through a fine sieve into a bowl. Refrigerate the purée until it is cool, then stir in the yogurt.

Whip the cream until it forms stiff peaks. Fold the whipped cream into the raspberry mixture.

Beat the egg whites in a bowl until stiff peaks form when the beater is lifted from the bowl. Fold the egg whites into the raspberry mixture.

Fill each of eight wine glasses with the raspberry mousse. Chill the glasses for at least 30 minutes; just before serving, garnish each mousse with three of the reserved raspberries.

Chilled Lemon Mousse with Blueberries

Serves 8
Working time: about 35 minutes
Total time: about 1 hour and 30 minutes

Calories **213**
Protein **3g.**
Cholesterol **50mg.**
Total fat **7g.**
Saturated fat **4g.**
Sodium **44mg.**

2 lemons
1 egg, plus 1 egg white
1 cup sugar
4 tbsp. unsalted butter, melted
3 cups fresh blueberries, picked over and rinsed
4 egg whites
⅛ tsp. cream of tartar
2 tbsp. sugar

Grate the zest of the lemons and put it in the top of a double boiler. Squeeze the juice from the lemons and add it to the zest. Whisk the egg, egg white and sugar into the lemon mixture, and set it over simmering water. Cook the mixture, stirring continuously, until it thickens — 12 to 15 minutes. (Do not overcook the mixture or it will curdle.)

Remove the double boiler from the heat and mix in the butter. Set the top of the double boiler in a larger bowl filled with ice and let the mixture cool, whisking it occasionally.

To prepare the meringue, put the egg whites and the cream of tartar into a bowl, and beat them until soft peaks form. Add a little of the sugar and continue beating the egg whites, gradually adding the remaining sugar, until stiff peaks have formed and the meringue is glossy.

Stir about ½ cup of the meringue into the cooled lemon mixture to lighten it. Fold in the remaining meringue and all but ½ cup of the blueberries. Spoon the lemon mousse into parfait glasses and chill the glasses for at least an hour before serving. Garnish each serving with a few of the reserved blueberries.

Layered Bavarian

Serves 8
Working time: about 1 hour
Total time: about 4 hours and 30 minutes
(includes chilling)

Calories **187**
Protein **10g.**
Cholesterol **5mg.**
Total fat **2g.**
Saturated fat **1g.**
Sodium **86mg.**

1 lb. ripe apricots or nectarines
1 tbsp. fresh lemon juice
3 tbsp. unflavored powdered gelatin
3 cups plain low-fat yogurt
2 tbsp. honey
1 tsp. pure vanilla extract
2 cups fresh blueberries, picked over and stemmed, or frozen whole blueberries, thawed
1 tbsp. fresh lime juice
3 egg whites
½ cup sugar
3 apricots, or 2 nectarines, thinly sliced, for garnish (optional)

Bring 4 quarts of water to a boil in a large pot. Add the apricots or nectarines and blanch them until their skins loosen — 30 seconds to one minute. Remove the apricots or nectarines from the water; when they are cool enough to handle, peel them and cut them in half, discarding the pits and skins. Purée the halves with the lemon juice in a food processor or a blender.

Pour 2 tablespoons of water into a small saucepan. Sprinkle in 1 tablespoon of the gelatin. Heat the mixture over low heat, stirring continuously until the gelatin has dissolved. Blend the gelatin mixture and ½ cup of the yogurt into the fruit purée. Set the mixture aside.

In a bowl, combine 2 cups of the remaining yogurt with the honey and vanilla. Pour 2 tablespoons of water into a small saucepan and sprinkle in 1 tablespoon of the remaining gelatin. Heat the mixture over low heat to dissolve the gelatin, then whisk it into the yogurt-honey mixture. Set this mixture aside.

Heat the blueberries and lime juice in a small, nonreactive saucepan over medium heat until the berries burst and render their juice — about five minutes. Purée the berries and juice in a food processor or a blender, then strain the purée through a fine sieve.

Pour 2 tablespoons of water into a small saucepan; sprinkle in the remaining tablespoon of gelatin, and heat the mixture over low heat until the gelatin dissolves. Blend this gelatin mixture and the remaining ½ cup of yogurt into the blueberry purée. Set the blueberry mixture aside.

Pour the egg whites into a deep bowl. Set up an electric mixer; you will need to start beating the egg whites as soon as the sugar is ready.

To prepare Italian meringue (technique, below), heat the sugar with ¼ cup of water in a small saucepan over medium-high heat. Boil the mixture until the bubbles rise to the surface in a random pattern, indicating that the water has nearly evaporated and the sugar itself is beginning to cook.

With a small spoon, drop a bit of the sugar into a bowl of ice water. If the sugar dissolves instantly, continue cooking it. When the sugar dropped into the water can be rolled between your fingers into a supple ball, begin beating the egg whites on high speed. Pour the sugar down the side of the bowl in a thin, steady stream. When all the sugar has been incorporated, decrease the speed to medium; continue beating the ▶

Making Italian Meringue

1 *TESTING THE SYRUP. In a heavy-bottomed pan, melt sugar until the surface bubbles continuously. To test for the "soft-ball" stage, drop a spoonful into ice water. Gather a ball of the cooled syrup with your fingers and remove it from the water. The ball should hold together yet feel pliable and sticky. (The soft-ball stage is reached between 234° and 240° F. on a candy thermometer.)*

2 *POURING IN THE SYRUP. As soon as the sugar has reached the soft-ball stage, start beating the egg whites at high speed in a bowl. Pour the hot syrup into the bowl in a slow, steady stream, avoiding the beater heads. After the syrup has been added, reduce the mixer speed to medium.*

3 *TESTING THE MERINGUE. Keep beating the mixture on medium until it cools to room temperature: Test the temperature by feeling the sides of the bowl with your hand. Then beat the mixture at high speed for one minute to stiffen it. The mixture will have frothed into a smooth, thick meringue and should hold stiff, glossy peaks.*

egg whites until they are glossy, have formed stiff peaks and have cooled to room temperature — at least five minutes. Increase the speed to high and beat the meringue for one minute more.

Fold one third of the meringue into each of the prepared mixtures. Do not refrigerate any of the mixtures.

Rinse an 8-cup mold under cold running water. Shake it dry; to facilitate unmolding the finished dessert, do not wipe it dry. Pour the apricot or nectarine mixture into the mold and refrigerate it for 45 minutes. Next, pour in the vanilla mixture and refrigerate the mold for 45 minutes more. Finally, pour the blueberry mixture into the mold, forming the third layer, and chill the mold in the refrigerator for at least two hours.

Unmold the Bavarian as close to serving time as possible: Dip the bottom of the mold into hot water for 15 seconds, then run the tip of a knife around the inside edge of the mold to break the air lock. Invert a chilled platter on top, and turn both platter and mold over together. If the Bavarian does not come free, wrap the mold in a towel that has been soaked with hot water and wrung out. After 15 seconds, remove the towel and lift away the mold. If you like, garnish the Bavarian with apricot or nectarine slices.

Orange and Buttermilk Parfaits

Serves 8
Working time: about 40 minutes
Total time: about 1 hour and 10 minutes

Calories **144**
Protein **5g.**
Cholesterol **70mg.**
Total fat **2g.**
Saturated fat **1g.**
Sodium **73mg.**

1½ cups buttermilk
½ tbsp. unflavored powdered gelatin
¾ cup sugar
2 eggs, separated, plus 1 egg white
¼ cup frozen orange-juice concentrate, thawed
2 navel oranges, for garnish

Put 1 cup of the buttermilk, the gelatin, ¼ cup of the sugar and the egg yolks into a small, heavy-bottomed saucepan over low heat. Cook the mixture, stirring constantly with a wooden spoon, until it is thick enough to coat the back of the spoon — six to eight minutes. (Do not let the mixture come to a boil or it will curdle.) Divide the mixture between two bowls. Whisk the remaining ½ cup of buttermilk into one of the bowls; whisk the orange-juice concentrate into the other. Set both bowls aside at room temperature.

Make Italian meringue (technique, page 87). First, pour the egg whites into a deep bowl. Then set up an electric mixer; you will need to start beating the egg whites as soon as the sugar is ready.

Heat the remaining ½ cup of sugar with ¼ cup of water in a small, heavy-bottomed saucepan over medium-high heat. Boil the mixture until the bubbles rise to the surface in a random pattern, indicating that the water has nearly evaporated and the sugar itself is beginning to cook. With a small spoon, drop a bit of the sugar into a bowl filled with ice water. If the sugar dissolves immediately, continue cooking. When the sugar dropped into the water can be rolled between your fingers into a supple ball, start the mixer.

Begin beating the egg whites at high speed. Pour the sugar into the bowl in a very thin, steady stream. When all the sugar has been incorporated, decrease the speed to medium; continue beating until the egg whites are glossy, have formed stiff peaks and have cooled to room temperature. Increase the speed to high and beat the meringue for one minute more.

Mix about ½ cup of the meringue into each of the buttermilk mixtures to lighten them. Fold half of the remaining meringue into each mixture.

Spoon the mixture containing the extra buttermilk into eight glasses and top it with the orange mixture. Refrigerate the parfaits for at least 30 minutes.

For the garnish, segment the two oranges (technique, page 14). Just before serving, garnish each portion with orange segments.

Raspberry Soufflés

Serves 6
Working time: about 50 minutes
Total time: about 1 hour and 10 minutes

Calories **45**
Protein **0g.**
Cholesterol **0mg.**
Total fat **0g.**
Saturated fat **0g.**
Sodium **6mg.**

½ cup plus 2 tbsp. sugar
2 cups fresh or frozen whole raspberries, thawed
2 egg whites
⅓ cup confectioners' sugar

Lightly butter six 4-ounce ramekins. Divide 2 tablespoons of the sugar evenly among the ramekins, then tilt and rotate the ramekins to coat them thoroughly with the sugar. Set the ramekins on a baking sheet and refrigerate them.

Purée the raspberries in a food processor or a blender. Strain the purée through a fine sieve and set it aside. Preheat the oven to 400° F.

Pour the egg whites into a deep bowl. Set up an electric mixer; you will need to start beating the egg whites as soon as the sugar is ready.

To prepare Italian meringue (technique, page 87), heat the remaining ½ cup of sugar with ¼ cup of water in a small saucepan over medium-high heat. Boil the mixture until the bubbles rise to the surface in a random pattern, indicating that the water has nearly evaporated and the sugar itself is beginning to cook.

With a small spoon, drop a bit of the sugar into a bowl of ice water. If the sugar dissolves immediately, continue cooking. When the sugar dropped into the water can be rolled between your fingers into a supple ball, begin beating the egg whites on high speed. Pour the sugar down the side of the bowl in a very thin, steady stream. When all the sugar has been incorporated, decrease the speed to medium; continue beating the egg whites until they are glossy, have formed stiff peaks and have cooled to room temperature — five to 10 minutes. Increase the speed to high and beat the meringue for one minute more.

Stir about one third of the meringue into the raspberry purée to lighten it, then fold in the remaining meringue. Divide the soufflé mixture among the prepared ramekins, slightly overfilling each one. Level their tops with a spatula, then run the tip of your thumb around the inside edge of each ramekin; the resulting circular depression will keep the edges of the soufflés from burning as the desserts puff up in the oven. Sift a little of the confectioners' sugar over the top of each soufflé; bake the soufflés until they have risen and are set — about 10 minutes. Serve the soufflés immediately.

EDITOR'S NOTE: *If it is inconvenient to serve the finished soufflés at once, keep them from collapsing by leaving them in the oven with the heat turned off and the door open.*

Mile-High Pie with Two Sauces

Serves 12
Working time: about 1 hour
Total time: about 2 hours

Calories **240**
Protein **6g.**
Cholesterol **71mg.**
Total fat **3g.**
Saturated fat **1g.**
Sodium **85mg.**

1 tbsp. safflower oil
1½ cups plus 2 tbsp. sugar
12 egg whites
1 tbsp. pure vanilla extract
¼ tsp. cream of tartar
Vanilla-yogurt sauce
1¼ cups low-fat milk
1 vanilla bean
3 egg yolks
2 tbsp. sugar
1 cup plain low-fat yogurt
Cranberry sauce
2 cups fresh or frozen cranberries, picked over
½ cup sugar
½ cup ruby port
⅓ cup plain low-fat yogurt

Brush the inside of a 9-inch springform pan with the oil. Sprinkle in 2 tablespoons of the sugar; shake and tilt the pan to coat it evenly with the sugar. Preheat the oven to 300° F.

To prepare the meringue, put the egg whites, vanilla extract and cream of tartar into a bowl. Begin beating the whites at low speed, gradually increasing the speed to medium as the whites turn opaque. Add the remaining 1½ cups of sugar a tablespoon at a time, increasing the beater speed all the while. When all the sugar has been incorporated, continue beating the whites on high speed until they are glossy and form stiff peaks when the beater is lifted from the bowl.

Transfer the meringue to the springform pan. Smooth the top of the meringue with a long spatula or the dull side of a knife. Bake the pie until it has risen and is lightly browned — about 40 minutes. It will be moist throughout. Remove the pie from the oven and let it cool to room temperature in the pan.

While the pie is baking and cooling, make the sauces. To make the vanilla-yogurt sauce, heat the milk, vanilla bean, egg yolks and sugar in a small, heavy-bottomed, nonreactive saucepan set over low heat. Cook the mixture, stirring constantly with a wooden spoon, until it is thick enough to coat the back of the spoon. Strain the sauce into a bowl and set it aside; when it has cooled to room temperature, whisk in the yogurt.

To make the cranberry sauce, combine the cranber-ries, sugar and ½ cup of water in a small saucepan over medium-high heat. Cook the cranberries until they burst — six to eight minutes. Continue cooking the berries until they are quite soft — about five minutes.

Press the cooked berries through a sieve into a bowl and set them aside. When they have cooled to room temperature, whisk in the port and the yogurt.

Just before serving the pie, remove the sides of the pan. With a wet knife, cut the pie into wedges; present them with the vanilla-yogurt sauce and the cranberry sauce poured around them. If you like, swirl the two sauces together as shown below.

Two Methods for Swirling Sauces

A Carousel of Hearts

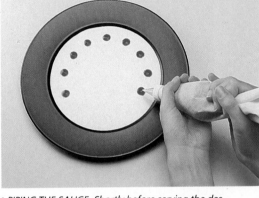

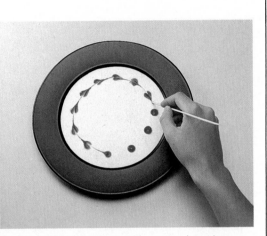

1 PIPING THE SAUCE. Shortly before serving the dessert, pour sauce into the center of a plate. Tip and swirl the plate to cover the bottom evenly. Pour sauce of a contrasting color into a pastry bag with a very small plain tip, as here, or into a plastic squirt bottle. Pipe a ring of dots onto the first sauce (above).

2 CONNECTING THE DOTS. With one steady motion, draw the blunt end of a wooden skewer or pick from the center of one dot through the center of the next dot in the ring. Continue connecting the dots, without lifting the skewer, until you have formed a wreath of linked hearts. Set the dessert in the middle.

A Rippled Kaleidoscope

1 CREATING A SPIRAL. Fill a plate with sauce as described above in Step 1. Pour a sauce of contrasting color into a plastic squirt bottle, as here, or into a pastry bag with a very small plain tip. Practice an even flow by squeezing some of the sauce onto a paper towel in a smooth line. Starting at the center of the plate, squeeze out the sauce in a continuous spiral.

2 RIPPLING THE SPIRAL. Draw the blunt end of a wooden skewer or pick from the center of the spiral to its rim. Lift the skewer from the surface of the sauce, reinsert it about an inch farther along the rim, and draw the skewer from the rim to the center. Repeat the process to divide the spiral into about a dozen rippled wedges of equal size. Set the dessert in the middle of the design.

Put the egg whites into a deep bowl. Set up an electric mixer; you will need to start beating the egg whites as soon as the sugar is ready.

To prepare Italian meringue (technique, page 87), heat the remaining ¼ cup of sugar with 2 tablespoons of water in a small saucepan over medium-high heat. Boil the mixture until the bubbles rise to the surface in a random pattern, indicating that the water has nearly evaporated and the sugar is beginning to cook.

With a small spoon, drop a bit of the sugar into a bowl filled with ice water. If the sugar dissolves immediately, continue cooking the sugar mixture. When the sugar dropped into the water can be rolled between your fingers into a supple ball, begin beating the egg whites on high speed. Pour the sugar down the side of the bowl in a thin, steady stream. When all the sugar has been incorporated, decrease the speed to medium; continue beating until the egg whites are glossy, have formed stiff peaks and have cooled to room temperature — about 10 minutes. Increase the speed to high and beat the meringue for one minute more.

Line an 8-inch cake pan with plastic wrap. Drain the raisins and scatter them in the bottom of the pan.

Mix about ⅓ of the meringue into the cheese mixture to lighten it. Gently fold in the rest of the meringue, then pour the cheesecake mixture into the lined pan. Chill the cheesecake for four hours.

To turn out the cheesecake, invert a serving plate on top of the pan, then turn both over together. Lift away the pan, peel off the plastic wrap, and slice the cheesecake for serving.

Raisin Cheesecake

Serves 12
Working time: about 1 hour
Total time: about 5 hours (includes chilling)

Calories **120**
Protein **7g.**
Cholesterol **11mg.**
Total fat **3g.**
Saturated fat **2g.**
Sodium **150mg.**

¼ cup golden raisins
¼ cup dark raisins
1 cup plain low-fat yogurt
3 oz. cream cheese
1 ¼ cups low-fat cottage cheese
1 tsp. pure vanilla extract
½ cup sugar
½ cup low-fat milk
1 tbsp. unflavored powdered gelatin
3 egg whites, at room temperature

Put all the raisins in a small bowl and pour 1 cup of hot water over them. Set the bowl aside.

Purée the yogurt, cream cheese, cottage cheese, vanilla and ¼ cup of the sugar in a food processor or a blender. Scrape the cheese mixture into a large bowl.

Pour the milk into a small saucepan. Sprinkle the gelatin over the milk and let it stand until the gelatin softens — about five minutes. Heat the milk over medium heat, stirring until the gelatin is dissolved. Stir the milk into the cheese mixture and set it aside.

Homemade Yogurt

Makes 1 quart
Working time: about 20 minutes
Total time: about 3 hours and 20 minutes

Per cup:
Calories **232**
Protein **13g.**
Cholesterol **20mg.**
Total fat **5g.**
Saturated fat **3g.**
Sodium **227mg.**

¾ cup nonfat dry milk
1 quart low-fat milk
3 tbsp. plain low-fat yogurt

Combine the dry milk and the low-fat milk, stirring until the dry milk is completely dissolved. Gently heat the milk until it registers between 110° and 115° F. on a dairy thermometer or a rapid-response thermometer, then remove it from the heat. Stir a little of the warm milk into the yogurt to temper it, then add the yogurt to the remaining warm milk. Gently stir the mixture until it is smooth; pour it into two clean one-pint jars. Cover the jars tightly and put them in a warm place — on top of your refrigerator for example; 90° F. is ideal — for three to five hours.

To test the yogurt for doneness, tilt one of the jars; the liquid whey should have separated from the solid curd. Press the curd with your finger — it should be firm. If the yogurt is still semiliquid, return the jar to the warm place until the curd sets. Pour off the whey, then cover the jars and store them in the refrigerator.

Blackberry Timbales with Almond Cream

Serves 8
Working time: about 45 minutes
Total time: about 2 hours and 45 minutes
(includes chilling)

Calories **278**
Protein **9g.**
Cholesterol **28mg.**
Total fat **8g.**
Saturated fat **5g.**
Sodium **168mg.**

5 tsp. unflavored powdered gelatin (2 envelopes)
1 pint blackberries (about 2 cups)
⅔ cup sugar
¼ tsp. salt
2 cups plain low-fat yogurt
¼ cup fresh lime juice
6 tbsp. amaretto
Almond cream
1½ cups low-fat milk
4 egg whites
½ cup heavy cream
¼ cup sugar
½ tsp. pure vanilla extract
⅛ tsp. almond extract
2 tbsp. amaretto
2 limes, thinly sliced, for garnish

To prepare the timbales, sprinkle the gelatin over ¼ cup of water in a measuring cup and let it soften for five minutes. Purée all but eight of the blackberries in a food processor or a blender. Strain the purée into a heavy-bottomed nonreactive saucepan. Stir the sugar, salt and softened gelatin into the purée. Warm the purée over low heat, stirring occasionally, until the gelatin and sugar melt — two to three minutes. Transfer the purée to a bowl.

In another bowl, whisk together the yogurt, lime juice and amaretto. Pour this mixture into the blackberry purée, whisking constantly. Tap the bottom of the bowl on the work surface to collapse any large air bubbles, then spoon the mixture into eight fluted timbale molds or individual gelatin molds. Refrigerate the timbales until they have set — about two hours.

While the timbales are chilling, prepare the almond cream. Bring 1 cup of the milk to a boil in a clean heavy-bottomed saucepan, then immediately remove the pan from the heat. Whisk the egg whites in a clean bowl until they are frothy. Add the cream, the sugar and the remaining ½ cup of unheated milk. Whisking constantly, slowly pour the hot milk into the egg-white mixture in a thin, steady stream; pouring slowly keeps the egg whites from forming clumps. Return the mixture to the saucepan in which you heated the milk. Stirring constantly, thicken the sauce over medium heat until it coats the back of the spoon — four to five minutes. Remove the saucepan from the heat; stir in the vanilla, almond extract and amaretto. Transfer the sauce to a bowl. Lay a sheet of plastic wrap directly on the surface of the sauce to prevent its forming a skin, and put the sauce into the refrigerator until it is ▶

chilled — about two hours.

To unmold a timbale, briefly dip the bottom of the mold in warm water. Invert a dessert plate over the mold, then turn the two over together, and lift away the mold. Repeat the process to unmold the other timbales. Spoon some of the sauce around each timbale and garnish each plate with a slice of lime and one whole blackberry.

Spiced Pumpkin Mousse with Lemon Cream

Serves 6
Working time: about 30 minutes
Total time: about 2 hours (includes chilling)

Calories **140**
Protein **4g.**
Cholesterol **18mg.**
Total fat **5g.**
Saturated fat **3g.**
Sodium **88mg.**

2½ tsp. unflavored powdered gelatin (1 envelope)
⅓ cup sugar
2 tsp. grated lemon zest
¾ tsp. anise seeds, finely ground
⅛ tsp. grated nutmeg
1 tbsp. finely chopped crystallized ginger
⅛ tsp. salt
1 cup canned pumpkin
¼ cup fresh lemon juice
4 egg whites, at room temperature
⅛ tsp. cream of tartar
Lemon cream
¼ cup julienned lemon zest
2 tbsp. sugar
2 tbsp. fresh lemon juice
⅓ cup heavy cream

Put ¼ cup of cold water into a bowl, then sprinkle in the gelatin. Let the gelatin soften for five minutes; pour in ¼ cup of boiling water and stir to dissolve the gelatin. Stir in the sugar, lemon zest, ground anise, nutmeg, ginger and salt. Add the pumpkin and lemon juice, and stir to combine them. Chill the mixture in the refrigerator, stirring occasionally, until it starts to gel — about 30 minutes.

When the pumpkin mixture is ready, beat the egg whites with the cream of tartar in a bowl until they form stiff peaks. Remove the pumpkin mixture from the refrigerator and whisk it vigorously for 15 seconds. Stir in one third of the egg whites and combine them thoroughly, then fold in the remaining egg whites *(technique, page 95)*.

Divide the mousse into six portions, mounding each one in the center, and chill them for one to six hours.

For the lemon cream, first put the zest in a small, nonreactive saucepan with ¼ cup of water, the 2 tablespoons of sugar and the 2 tablespoons of lemon juice. Bring the liquid to a boil, then reduce the heat to low, and simmer the mixture until it becomes a thick syrup — about five minutes. Strain the syrup into a small bowl, reserving the zest. Set half of the cooked zest aside; finely chop the rest.

Just before serving, whip the cream in a small bowl. Fold in the syrup and the finely chopped lemon zest. Garnish each mousse with a dollop of the lemon cream and a few strands of the reserved julienned zest.

Folding Mixtures Together

1 *LIGHTENING THE MIXTURE. To ensure an airy dessert's lightness, add one fourth to one third of the lighter mixture (here, beaten egg whites) to the heavier one (in this instance, pumpkin purée) and whisk them gently together. This will lighten the mixture enough so that the remaining egg whites can be folded in easily.*

2 *ADDING THE EGG WHITES. Scoop the remaining beaten egg whites into the bowl containing the lightened mixture. With the blade of a rubber spatula, cut down through the center.*

3 *FOLDING. Glide the spatula across the bottom of the bowl, then lift and turn over the purée and egg whites as you reach the edge. Give the bowl a quarter turn. Continue cutting, lifting and turning the mixture, rotating the bowl each time, until the egg whites have been evenly incorporated.*

Indian Pudding with Buttermilk Cream

Serves 8
Working time: about 25 minutes
Total time: about 2 hours

Calories **231**
Protein **8g.**
Cholesterol **13mg.**
Total fat **3g.**
Saturated fat **2g.**
Sodium **126mg.**

¾ cup stone-ground yellow cornmeal
1 tsp. ground cinnamon
1 tsp. ground ginger
4 cups low-fat milk
½ cup molasses
1 tsp. pure vanilla extract
Buttermilk cream
2 tbsp. cornstarch
¼ cup sugar
1 cup low-fat milk
1 cup buttermilk
1 tsp. pure vanilla extract

Preheat the oven to 325° F.

Combine the cornmeal, cinnamon, ginger and 1 cup of the milk in a heatproof bowl. Pour the remaining 3 cups of milk into a saucepan and bring the milk to a boil. Stirring constantly, pour the hot milk into the cornmeal mixture in a thin, steady stream.

Transfer the cornmeal mixture to the saucepan; stirring continuously, bring it to a boil. Reduce the heat to medium low and cook the mixture, stirring constantly, until it has the consistency of a thick sauce — about three minutes more. Stir in the molasses and the vanilla extract, then pour the cornmeal mixture into a baking dish, and bake it until it sets — about one hour.

While the pudding is baking, make the buttermilk cream. Mix the cornstarch and sugar in a small saucepan, then whisk in the low-fat milk. Bring the mixture to a boil and cook it for one minute. Remove the pan from the heat and stir in the buttermilk and vanilla. Transfer the buttermilk cream to a bowl and chill it in the refrigerator.

Remove the pudding from the oven and allow it to cool at room temperature for about 45 minutes; just before serving, top the pudding with the chilled buttermilk cream.

Orange Chiffon Cheesecake

Serves 12
Working time: about 1 hour
Total time: about 1 day (includes chilling)

Calories **145**
Protein **7g.**
Cholesterol **12mg.**
Total fat **4g.**
Saturated fat **2g.**
Sodium **130mg.**

1 cup sugar
2 navel oranges, peeled, halved lengthwise and cut crosswise into ⅛-inch-thick slices
½ cup fresh orange juice
2½ tbsp. fresh lemon juice
2½ tsp. unflavored powdered gelatin (1 envelope)
1 cup part-skim ricotta cheese
1 cup low-fat cottage cheese
2 oz. cream cheese
grated zest of 1 orange
grated zest of 1 lemon
3 egg whites

Put the sugar and ½ cup of water into a saucepan. Bring the mixture to a boil, then add the orange slices,

reduce the heat, and simmer the oranges for 20 minutes. Refrigerate the oranges in the syrup for one hour.

Pour the orange juice and lemon juice into a small saucepan. Sprinkle in the gelatin, then set the pan aside until the gelatin has softened.

Meanwhile, purée the ricotta, cottage cheese, cream cheese, orange zest and lemon zest in a food processor or a blender until they are very smooth. Transfer the cheese mixture to a bowl.

Set the saucepan containing the gelatin mixture over low heat; cook it, stirring continuously, until the gelatin has dissolved. Stir the gelatin mixture into the puréed cheeses.

Remove the orange slices from their syrup and drain them on paper towels. Reserve the syrup.

Pour the egg whites into a deep bowl. Set up an electric mixer; you will need to start beating the egg whites as soon as the sugar is ready.

To prepare Italian meringue *(technique, page 87),*

heat the reserved syrup in a small saucepan over medium-high heat. Boil the mixture until the bubbles rise to the surface in a random pattern, indicating that the liquid has nearly evaporated and the sugar itself is beginning to cook.

With a small spoon, drop a bit of the syrup into a bowl filled with ice water. If the sugar dissolves immediately, continue cooking the sugar mixture. When the sugar dropped into the water can be rolled between your fingers into a supple ball, begin beating the egg whites on high speed. Pour the sugar down the side of the bowl in a very thin, steady stream. When all the sugar has been incorporated, decrease the speed to medium; continue beating the egg whites until they are glossy, have formed stiff peaks and have cooled to room temperature. Increase the speed to high and beat the meringue for one minute more.

Mix about one quarter of the meringue into the cheese mixture to lighten it, then gently fold in the rest. Rinse a 6-cup ring mold with cold water and shake out the excess. (Do not wipe the mold dry; the clinging moisture will help the dessert unmold cleanly.) Line the mold with the drained orange slices, then pour in the cheesecake mixture, and chill it in the refrigerator for four hours.

To turn out the cheesecake, invert a chilled platter on top of the mold and turn both over together. Wrap the bottom of the mold in a towel that has been soaked with hot water and wrung out. After five seconds, remove the towel and lift away the mold.

Kugel with Dried Fruit

Serves 12
Working time: about 35 minutes
Total time: about 1 hour and 35 minutes

Calories **327**
Protein **13g.**
Cholesterol **17mg.**
Total fat **6g.**
Saturated fat **3g.**
Sodium **231mg.**

½ lb. dried wide egg noodles
1 cup sugar
1 lb. low-fat cottage cheese
½ lb. farmer cheese
1 cup plain low-fat yogurt
1 tsp. pure vanilla extract
2 tbsp. fresh lemon juice
1 cup golden raisins
½ cup diced dried pears
½ cup diced dried apples
½ cup diced dried prunes
2 tbsp. cornstarch
2 cups low-fat milk
2 tbsp. dry bread crumbs
Cinnamon topping
2 tbsp. unsalted butter, softened
½ cup dry bread crumbs
½ tsp. ground cinnamon
2 tbsp. sugar

Add the noodles to 3 quarts of boiling water. Start testing for doneness after seven minutes and continue cooking the noodles until they are *al dente*. Drain the noodles and rinse them under cold running water, then set them aside.

Preheat the oven to 350° F. In a large bowl, mix together the sugar, cottage cheese, farmer cheese, yogurt, vanilla, lemon juice, raisins, pears, apples and prunes. Dissolve the cornstarch in ½ cup of the milk. Stir the cornstarch mixture and the remaining 1½ cups of milk into the cheese mixture.

Stir the noodles together with the cheese mixture, coating them well. Lightly oil a nonreactive 9- by 13-inch baking dish and coat it with the 2 tablespoons of bread crumbs. Transfer the noodles to the baking dish.

To make the cinnamon topping, mix together the butter, the ½ cup of bread crumbs, the cinnamon and the sugar. Sprinkle the topping over the noodles, then cover the dish with foil, and bake it for 30 minutes. Remove the foil and bake the kugel until it is golden brown — about 30 minutes more.

4

Festive Treats to Finish a Meal

With a knowing choice of ingredients and with the right preparation techniques, pies, pastries, cakes and cookies that are ordinarily laden with fat and calories can be brought within the bounds of healthful eating. What is more, this can be accomplished without sacrificing the flavors that make such confections so appealing. Two staples of traditional dessert cookery — butter and egg yolks — have a place in the doughs and batters in this section, but they form a relatively small proportion of a recipe's total ingredients. Although the dough for cream puffs has always been made with whole eggs, replacing some of the egg yolks with egg whites, it turns out, still produces a light and billowing puff *(page 103)*.

The familiar all-purpose and cake flours figure in many of the following recipes, but others incorporate flours and grains with greater nutritional value. Whole-wheat flour lends an earthy undertone and added fiber to orange beet cake, a variation on carrot cake and zucchini bread. The dessert crepes on page 100 feature high-protein buckwheat flour. When fruit is used, as in the apple-rhubarb pastries on page 107 or the pear tart on page 120, there can be a bonus of vitamins, minerals and fiber.

Some of the 25 desserts in this section are based on stiffly beaten egg whites and sugar, which, of course, contain no fat at all. Among these are the crisply baked, snow-white meringue baskets on page 124, ideal for filling with fresh fruit. Beaten egg whites also leaven three kinds of cake — angel food, sponge and chiffon — presented here in new guises. After beating the whites to the desired consistency, finish the recipe promptly and transfer the dessert to the oven without delay; if allowed to stand, the egg-white foam would begin to dry out and lose its flexibility.

Apple-Filled Buckwheat Crepes with Cider Syrup

Serves 4
Working time: about 1 hour
Total time: about 1 hour and 30 minutes

Calories **322**
Protein **4g.**
Cholesterol **71mg.**
Total fat **11g.**
Saturated fat **2g.**
Sodium **93mg.**

2 cups unsweetened apple cider
1 lb. sweet apples
¼ tsp. ground cinnamon
2 tbsp. sour cream
Crepe batter
¼ cup buckwheat flour
½ cup unbleached all-purpose flour
⅛ tsp. salt
1 egg
2 tbsp. plus ¼ tsp. safflower oil

To prepare the crepe batter, sift together the buckwheat flour, all-purpose flour and salt. In a large bowl, whisk together the egg, 2 tablespoons of the oil and ¼ cup of water. Gradually whisk in the sifted ingredients until a smooth mixture results. Cover the bowl and refrigerate the batter for at least one hour.

Bring 1½ cups of the apple cider to a boil in a heavy-bottomed saucepan. Lower the heat to medium low and boil the cider until it is reduced to ¼ cup — 20 to 30 minutes. Set the apple syrup aside.

Peel, quarter and core the apples, then cut the quarters into ½-inch pieces. Combine the apple pieces with the cinnamon and the remaining ½ cup of apple cider in a large, heavy-bottomed skillet set over medium heat. Cook the apple mixture, stirring occasionally, until almost all of the liquid has evaporated — 15 to 20 minutes. Transfer the apple mixture to a food processor or a blender, and purée it. Return the purée to the skillet and keep it in a warm place.

When the batter is chilled, heat a crepe pan or an 8-inch skillet over medium-high heat. Pour in the remaining ¼ teaspoon of oil; with a paper towel, wipe the oil over the pan's entire cooking surface. Pour 2 to 3 tablespoons of the crepe batter into the hot pan and immediately swirl the pan to coat the bottom with a thin, even layer of batter. Pour any excess batter back into the bowl. Cook the crepe until the bottom is browned — about 2 minutes and 30 seconds — then lift the edge with a spatula and turn the crepe over. Cook the crepe on the second side until it too is browned — 15 to 30 seconds — and slide the crepe onto a warmed plate. Repeat the process with the remaining batter to form eight crepes in all.

Spread about 3 tablespoons of the warm apple purée over each crepe. Fold each crepe in half, then fold it in half again to produce a wedge shape. Arrange two crepes, one slightly overlapping the other, on each of four dessert plates. Drizzle a tablespoon of the apple syrup over each serving; garnish each dessert with ½ tablespoon of the sour cream and serve at once.

Honey-Glazed Buttermilk Cake

Serves 16
Working time: about 30 minutes
Total time: about 2 hours and 30 minutes

Calories **273**
Protein **3g.**
Cholesterol **9mg.**
Total fat **6g.**
Saturated fat **2g.**
Sodium **126mg.**

3 cups cake flour
1 tsp. baking soda
2 ⅓ cups sugar
4 tbsp. unsalted butter, cut into ½-inch-thick pats
4 tbsp. corn-oil margarine, cut into ½-inch-thick pats
2 tsp. pure vanilla extract
1½ cups buttermilk
4 egg whites
grated zest of 1 lemon
Honey glaze
¼ cup sugar
¼ cup buttermilk
¼ cup honey
½ tsp. pure vanilla extract

Lightly butter a 12-cup Bundt pan, then dust it with flour. Preheat the oven to 325° F.

Mix the flour, baking soda and sugar in a bowl. With an electric mixer on the lowest speed, cut the butter and margarine into the dry ingredients until the mixture has the consistency of fine meal.

Stir together the vanilla, buttermilk and egg whites. Mix half of this liquid with the dry ingredients on medium-low speed for one minute. Add the remaining liquid and mix it in at medium speed for one minute more, scraping down the sides of the bowl as necessary. Stir in the grated lemon zest.

Pour the batter into the prepared Bundt pan. Bake the cake until it begins to pull away from the sides of the pan and feels springy to the touch — about 55 minutes. Set the cake aside to cool in the pan.

To make the glaze, combine the sugar, buttermilk and honey in a small saucepan. Bring the liquid to a boil over medium heat, then continue boiling it, stirring occasionally, until it is a light caramel color and has thickened slightly — about 10 minutes. (Although the buttermilk in the glaze will separate when the liquid first comes to a boil, the subsequent cooking will yield a smooth, well-blended sauce.)

Remove the saucepan from the heat; stir in the vanilla and 1 teaspoon of water. Let the mixture cool completely — it should be thick enough to coat the back of a spoon.

Invert the cooled cake onto a serving platter. Lift away the Bundt pan and pour the glaze over the cake, letting the glaze run down the sides.

Orange-Beet Cake

Serves 16
Working time: about 1 hour
Total time: about 1 hour and 45 minutes

Calories **188**
Protein **3g.**
Cholesterol **52mg.**
Total fat **6g.**
Saturated fat **1g.**
Sodium **113mg.**

⅓ cup golden raisins
⅓ cup dark raisins
1 cup fresh orange juice
¾ cup unbleached all-purpose flour
¾ cup whole-wheat flour
1 tsp. baking soda
¼ tsp. salt
1 tsp. ground cinnamon
1 tsp. grated nutmeg
3 eggs, separated, the whites at room temperature
⅓ cup safflower oil
1 tbsp. grated orange zest
1 tsp. pure vanilla extract
½ cup dark brown sugar
⅓ cup plain low-fat yogurt

3 beets, peeled and grated (about 1½ cups)
⅔ cup sugar

Put the golden raisins, dark raisins and orange juice into a nonreactive saucepan. Bring the juice to a boil, then reduce the heat, and simmer the mixture for five minutes. Drain the raisins in a sieve set over another nonreactive saucepan; reserve the juice and set the raisins aside. Return the juice to the heat and simmer it until only about 3 tablespoons remain — seven minutes or so.

Preheat the oven to 350° F.

Lightly oil a 9-inch springform pan. Line the base of the pan with a disk of parchment paper or wax paper, then lightly oil the paper, and dust the pan with flour.

Sift the all-purpose flour, whole-wheat flour, baking soda, salt, cinnamon and nutmeg into a bowl. In a separate bowl, whisk the egg yolks. Stir 1 tablespoon of the oil into the yolks. Whisking vigorously, blend in the remaining oil a tablespoon at a time. Continue whisking the yolks until the mixture is emulsified. Stir the orange zest, vanilla, brown sugar, yogurt, beets and raisins into the yolk mixture. Fold the flour mixture into the yolk mixture.

Beat the egg whites until soft peaks form. Sprinkle in the sugar and beat for one minute more. Stir one fourth of the beaten egg whites into the batter to lighten it, then gently fold the lightened batter into the remaining beaten egg whites. Pour the batter into the springform pan.

Bake the cake just until a knife inserted in the center comes out clean — 45 to 55 minutes. Remove the cake from the oven and let it cool for 10 minutes. Gently reheat the reserved orange juice and brush it over the top of the warm cake.

EDITOR'S NOTE: *This cake tastes even better two or three days after it has been baked. Store it in an airtight container.*

Cherry Puffs

Serves 12
Working time: about 1 hour and 10 minutes
Total time: about 2 hours

Calories **172**
Protein **5g.**
Cholesterol **74mg.**
Total fat **7g.**
Saturated fat **2g.**
Sodium **81mg.**

1½ lb. sweet cherries, pitted
grated zest of 4 lemons
½ cup fresh lemon juice
2 tbsp. cornstarch
¼ cup kirsch
¾ cup plain low-fat yogurt
2 tbsp. sugar
Chou-puff dough
2 tbsp. unsalted butter
2 tbsp. safflower oil
¼ tsp. salt
1 tsp. sugar
1 cup unbleached all-purpose flour
3 eggs, plus 2 egg whites

Combine the cherries, lemon zest and lemon juice in a saucepan over medium-high heat. Bring the mixture to a boil, then reduce the heat to maintain a simmer, and cook the mixture for five minutes. Combine the cornstarch with the kirsch in a small bowl and stir them into the cherry mixture. Continue cooking, stirring constantly, until the mixture thickens — about two minutes. Set the cherry filling aside at room temperature.

Whisk together the yogurt and sugar in a small bowl; refrigerate the bowl.

Preheat the oven to 425° F.

To make the chou-puff dough, combine the butter, oil, salt, sugar and 1 cup of water in a heavy-bottomed saucepan. Bring the mixture to a boil over medium-high heat. As soon as the butter melts, remove the pan from the heat and stir in the flour with a wooden spoon. Return the pan to the stove over medium heat; cook the mixture, stirring constantly, until it comes cleanly away from the sides of the pan and leaves a slight film on the bottom.

Remove the pan from the heat once more and allow it to cool for two minutes before adding the eggs. Incorporate the eggs one at a time, beating well after you add each one, until a smooth dough results. In a separate bowl, whisk the egg whites until they are frothy; beat one half of the egg whites into the dough. To test the consistency of the dough, scoop some up with a spoon, then turn the spoon and wait for the dough to fall off; it should fall off cleanly at the count of three. If it does not, beat more of the egg whites into the dough.

Spoon the dough into a pastry bag fitted with a ½-inch plain tip. Pipe the dough onto a lightly oiled baking sheet in 12 mounting swirls about 2 inches in diameter and 2 inches apart. (If you do not have a pastry bag, fashion the swirls with a spoon.) Bake the swirls until they puff up and are uniformly browned — about 25 minutes. Turn off the oven, prop the door ajar with the handle of a wooden spoon, and let the puffs dry in the oven for 15 minutes. Transfer the puffs to a rack to cool.

To assemble the puffs, slice each in half horizontally and spoon the cherry filling into the bottoms. Top each filling with a tablespoon of the sweetened yogurt; replace the tops and serve the puffs immediately.

Marbled Angel-Food Cake

Serves 12
Working time: about 25 minutes
Total time: about 2 hours and 30 minutes

Calories **128**
Protein **4g.**
Cholesterol **0mg.**
Total fat **0g.**
Saturated fat **0g.**
Sodium **65mg.**

½ cup plus 5 tbsp. unbleached all-purpose flour
3 tbsp. unsweetened cocoa powder
1 ¼ cups sugar
⅛ tsp. salt
10 egg whites
1 tsp. cream of tartar
½ tsp. almond extract
½ tsp. pure vanilla extract
1 tbsp. confectioners' sugar

Sift 5 tablespoons of the flour, the cocoa powder and 2 tablespoons of the sugar into a bowl. Sift the cocoa mixture three more times and set the bowl aside. Sift the remaining ½ cup of flour, the salt and 2 table-spoons of the remaining sugar into a second bowl. Sift this mixture three more times and set it aside too.

Preheat the oven to 350° F. Rinse out a tube pan and shake — do not wipe — it dry.

With an electric mixer, beat the egg whites until soft peaks form when the beater is lifted. Add the cream of tartar, then blend in the remaining cup of sugar a little at a time, beating the egg whites until they form stiff peaks. With the mixer set on the lowest speed, blend in the almond extract, then the vanilla. Transfer half of the beaten egg whites to a clean bowl.

Fold the dry cocoa mixture into the beaten egg whites in one bowl, then pour this chocolate batter into the tube pan. Fold the remaining dry mixture into the beaten egg whites in the other bowl, and spoon the batter over the chocolate batter in the tube pan. Plunge a spatula down through both layers of batter, then bring it back to the surface with a twisting motion. Repeat this step at 1-inch intervals around the cake to marble the batter thoroughly.

Bake the cake for 45 minutes. Invert the pan and let the cake cool for 90 minutes. Run a knife around the sides of the pan to loosen the cake before turning it out. Sift the confectioners' sugar over the cake.

Chocolate Chiffon Cake with Raspberry Filling

Serves 12
Working time: about 40 minutes
Total time: about 2 hours

Calories **207**
Protein **3g.**
Cholesterol **46mg.**
Total fat **6g.**
Saturated fat **1g.**
Sodium **112mg.**

¼ cup unsweetened cocoa powder
¾ cup cake flour
¾ cup sugar
1 tsp. baking soda
⅛ tsp. salt
¼ cup safflower oil
2 eggs, separated, plus 2 egg whites, the whites at room temperature
1 tsp. pure vanilla extract
¼ tsp. cream of tartar

Raspberry filling

2 cups fresh or frozen whole raspberries
½ cup sugar

Raspberry-Champagne sauce

2 cups fresh or frozen whole raspberries, thawed
½ tsp. fresh lemon juice
¾ cup chilled dry Champagne
2 tbsp. sugar (if you are using fresh raspberries)

Spoon the unsweetened cocoa powder into a small heatproof bowl and stir ½ cup of boiling water into it. Set the bowl aside.

Preheat the oven to 350° F.

Sift the flour, 6 tablespoons of the sugar, the baking soda and salt into a large bowl. Stir in the oil, egg yolks, the cocoa mixture and the vanilla; mix to blend the ingredients.

Pour the egg whites into a bowl and beat them until they are frothy. Add the cream of tartar, then continue beating the whites until soft peaks form. Gradually adding the remaining 6 tablespoons of sugar, beat the whites until they form stiff peaks.

Mix one third of the beaten whites into the flour mixture to lighten it; gently fold in the remaining whites. Pour the mixture into a 9-by-5-by-3-inch loaf pan. Bake the cake until a wooden pick inserted in the center comes out clean — about 55 minutes. Invert the pan on a cake rack and let the cake cool completely.

While the cake is cooling, make the raspberry filling. Combine the 2 cups of raspberries, ½ cup of sugar and ▶

2 tablespoons of water in a heavy saucepan over medium heat; cook the mixture, stirring constantly, until it has the consistency of fruit preserves — about 25 minutes. Refrigerate the filling.

For the sauce, purée the 2 cups of raspberries with the lemon juice in a food processor or a blender. (If you are using fresh raspberries, include the 2 tablespoons of sugar in the purée.) Strain the purée into a bowl; discard the solids. Refrigerate the purée.

Run a knife blade around the sides of the loaf pan, then invert the pan again and rap it sharply against the work surface to unmold the cake. Cut the cake into two horizontal layers. Spread the chilled raspberry filling over the bottom layer, then set the top layer back in place. Just before serving, stir the Champagne into the chilled raspberry purée. Cut the cake into serving slices, and surround each one with a little raspberry-Champagne sauce.

EDITOR'S NOTE: *If you are using Dutch-process cocoa powder, which is more alkaline than domestic brands, substitute 1½ teaspoons of baking powder for the teaspoon of baking soda. A split of Champagne will yield ¾ cup.*

Papaya Porcupines with Coconut Quills

Makes about 20 porcupines
Working time: about 30 minutes
Total time: about 45 minutes

Per porcupine:	
Calories **49**	2 egg whites
Protein **1g.**	2 tbsp. fresh lemon juice
Cholesterol **0mg.**	½ cup unbleached all-purpose flour
Total fat **1g.**	6 tbsp. sugar
Saturated fat **1g.**	⅔ cup sweetened dried coconut
Sodium **14mg.**	1 papaya (about 1 lb.), peeled and cut into about 20 chunks

Preheat the oven to 400° F.

Prepare the coating for the papaya: In a small bowl, thoroughly whisk the egg whites, lemon juice, flour and 2 tablespoons of the sugar. Set the coating aside.

Spread out the coconut on a sheet of wax paper.

Toss the papaya pieces with the remaining ¼ cup of sugar. Dip a piece of papaya into the coating, then hold the piece over the bowl to allow the excess coating to drip off. Roll the papaya piece in the coconut, then transfer it to a baking sheet. Repeat the process to coat the remaining pieces.

Bake the papaya porcupines until the coating has set and is lightly browned — about 15 minutes. Serve the papaya porcupines warm.

Rhubarb Tartlets
Topped with Meringue

Serves 4
Working (and total) time: about 1 hour and 30 minutes

Calories **202**
Protein **3g.**
Cholesterol **7mg.**
Total fat **5g.**
Saturated fat **2g.**
Sodium **180mg.**

1 tart green apple, peeled, cored and cut into ½-inch cubes
2 tbsp. dry white wine
1 lb. fresh rhubarb, trimmed and cut into ½-inch pieces, or 1 lb. frozen rhubarb, thawed
¼ cup light brown sugar
¼ tsp. pure vanilla extract
½ tbsp. fresh lemon juice
¼ tsp. ground cinnamon
grated nutmeg
⅛ tsp. salt
4 frozen phyllo-dough sheets in a stack, thawed
1 tbsp. unsalted butter, melted
1 egg white
1½ tbsp. sugar

Put the apple cubes and wine into a saucepan and simmer them, covered, for five minutes. Add the rhubarb, reduce the heat to low, and cook the mixture, uncovered, for five minutes more. Stir in the brown sugar, vanilla, lemon juice, cinnamon, a pinch of nutmeg and the salt. Continue cooking the mixture, stirring occasionally, until most of the liquid has evaporated — five to 10 minutes. Set the mixture aside.

Preheat the oven to 350° F.

To prepare the pastry, fold the stack of phyllo sheets in half, then fold it in half again and trim off the edges to produce a stack of sixteen 5-inch squares. Lay one of the phyllo squares on a work surface; using a pastry brush, lightly dab the square with a little of the melted butter. Set a second square atop the first and brush it with butter. Set a third square on top of the second at a 45-degree angle, forming an eight-pointed star. Dab the top of the third square with butter and cover it with a fourth square.

Lightly oil four cups of a muffin tin. Transfer the stacked phyllo to one of the cups and gently press it in place, taking care that the edges of the phyllo come as far as possible up the sides of the cup. Prepare the remaining phyllo squares in the same manner, making four tartlets in all.

Bake the tartlets until they are light brown and crisp — about eight minutes. Remove the muffin tin from the oven and unmold the tartlets, then set them aside. Let the tartlets cool to room temperature.

Increase the oven temperature to 500° F.

To make the meringue, whip the egg white in a small bowl until the white forms soft peaks. Continue beating, gradually adding the sugar, until stiff peaks form when the beater is lifted from the bowl.

Set the tartlets on a cookie sheet and divide the rhubarb mixture among them. Using a pastry bag or a spoon, top each with some of the meringue; bake the tartlets until the meringue browns — about three minutes. Serve the tartlets within two hours.

Oatmeal-Cocoa Kisses

Makes about 48 small cookies
Working time: about 30 minutes
Total time: about 4 hours and 30 minutes
(includes standing time)

Per cookie:
Calories **56**
Protein **1g.**
Cholesterol **0mg.**
Total fat **2g.**
Saturated fat **0g.**
Sodium **7mg.**

1¼ cups rolled oats
1 cup walnuts (about ¼ lb.)
¼ cup unsweetened cocoa powder
1 tbsp. fresh lemon juice
4 egg whites, at room temperature
¹⁄₁₆ tsp. salt
3 cups confectioners' sugar

Toast the rolled oats in a heavy-bottomed skillet over medium-high heat, stirring constantly, until they are lightly browned — about five minutes. Scrape the oats into a food processor or a blender; chop them until they have the texture of fine cornmeal. Add the nuts and process until the nuts are finely chopped. Transfer the oats and nuts to a bowl.

Stir the cocoa powder and lemon juice into the oat-nut mixture. In a separate bowl, beat the egg whites with the salt until soft peaks form. Gradually beat the confectioners' sugar into the whites until stiff peaks form. Stir the oat mixture into the beaten egg whites.

Spoon the cookie batter into a pastry bag fitted with a large star tip. Pipe ½ teaspoon of the batter onto each corner of two baking sheets. Line each sheet with parchment paper or wax paper, pressing down on the corners so that they stick to the batter. Pipe the remaining batter onto the baking sheets in mounds about 1 inch across, spacing them 1 inch apart. (If you do not have a pastry bag, drop scant tablespoonfuls of the batter onto the baking sheets.) Let the mounds stand and dry out at room temperature for three to four hours so that they will be crisp when baked.

At the end of the standing time, preheat the oven to 300° F. Bake the kisses until they are dry and slightly puffed — 20 to 25 minutes.

Crisp Oatmeal Cookies

Makes about 48 cookies
Working time: about 30 minutes
Total time: about 1 hour

Per cookie:
Calories **56**
Protein **1g.**
Cholesterol **11mg.**
Total fat **1g.**
Saturated fat **0g.**
Sodium **51mg.**

2 eggs, plus 1 egg white
1 tsp. ground cinnamon
1 tsp. pure vanilla extract
¼ tsp. salt
4 tsp. baking powder
1½ cups sugar
2 tbsp. safflower oil
3½ cups quick-cooking oatmeal

Line a baking sheet with aluminum foil. Preheat the oven to 375° F.

Put the eggs, cinnamon, vanilla, salt, baking powder and sugar in a bowl. Beat the mixture until it forms a ribbon when the beater is lifted from the bowl — about three minutes. With a wooden spoon, stir in the oil, then the oatmeal. (The mixture is too thick to be combined with an electric mixer.)

Drop rounded teaspoonfuls of the cookie dough onto the prepared baking sheet, leaving about 2 inches between cookies. Bake the cookies until they are golden brown — 10 to 12 minutes. The cookies will puff up at first, then sink down — a sign that they have nearly finished cooking.

Let the cookies cool to room temperature on the foil before attempting to remove them. Store the cookies in an airtight container.

Amaretti

SERVE THESE ALMOND COOKIES AS AN ACCOMPANIMENT TO
CREAMY DESSERTS AND SORBETS, OR ON THEIR OWN
WITH YOUR FAVORITE AFTER-DINNER BEVERAGE.

Makes about 100 cookies
Working time: about 30 minutes
Total time: about 9 hours (includes standing time)

Per cookie:
Calories **21**
Protein **0g.**
Cholesterol **0mg.**
Total fat **1g.**
Saturated fat **0g.**
Sodium **9mg.**

½ lb. almond paste
2 tsp. pure almond extract
1 cup sugar
4 egg whites
⅛ tsp. salt
confectioners' sugar

Mix together the almond paste, almond extract and ⅔
cup of the sugar in a bowl. Beating continuously,
gradually add about half of the egg whites. Continue
beating until the mixture has lightened in texture and
color — about three minutes.

To prepare the meringue, beat the remaining egg
whites in a bowl until they are foamy. Add the salt,
then continue beating the whites until they form soft
peaks. Gradually add the remaining ⅓ cup of sugar,
beating all the while, until the whites form stiff peaks.

Fold one third of the meringue into the almond mixture to lighten it, then fold in the remaining meringue.
Spoon the mixture into a pastry bag fitted with a plain
tip. Line two baking sheets with parchment paper and
pipe out the mixture in mounds about 1 inch across.
Sprinkle the mounds generously with confectioners'
sugar and let them stand at room temperature for at
least eight hours.

Preheat the oven to 350° F.

To allow the amaretti to puff during baking, pinch a
mound at its base, cracking the surface. Pinch the
mound once more to crack its surface a second time at
a right angle to the first. Repeat the process to crack
all the amaretti.

Bake the amaretti, with the oven door propped
slightly ajar with the handle of a wooden spoon, for 30
minutes. Remove the cookies from the oven and let
them stand, still on the parchment paper, until they
have cooled to room temperature. Remove the amaretti from the parchment paper, and store them in an
airtight container until serving time.

EDITOR'S NOTE: *The almond paste called for in this recipe is
available in supermarkets.*

Brandy Snaps

THESE COOKIES ARE DESIGNED TO DECORATE THE
APPLE MOUSSE CAKE ON PAGE 61. THEY ALSO MAKE A
DELIGHTFUL DESSERT WHEN SERVED ON THEIR OWN.

Makes 12 cookies
Working time: about 10 minutes
Total time: about 20 minutes

Per cookie:
Calories **54**
Protein **0g.**
Cholesterol **5mg.**
Total fat **2g.**
Saturated fat **1g.**
Sodium **3mg.**

2 tbsp. unsalted butter
2 tbsp. sugar
2 tbsp. light corn syrup
1 tsp. molasses
1 tsp. ground ginger
½ tsp. grated lemon zest
2 tbsp. brandy
⅓ cup unbleached all-purpose flour

Preheat the oven to 400° F.

Put all the ingredients but the flour into a small saucepan and bring the mixture to a boil. Cook the mixture for one minute, then remove it from the heat and let it cool for one minute. Add the flour and whisk the batter until it is smooth.

Lightly oil a heavy baking sheet. Drop the cookie batter onto the sheet in heaping teaspoonfuls at least 3 inches apart. (It may be necessary to bake the cookies in two batches; if you are using two baking sheets, stagger the cooking to allow enough time to shape the cookies after they are baked.) Bake the cookies until they turn slightly darker — three to four minutes.

Remove the baking sheet from the oven and let it sit for one minute while the cookies firm up a little. With a metal spatula, remove some of the still-soft cookies and drape them over a clean rolling pin to cool. Remove the curved cookies from the rolling pin as soon as they harden — about 30 seconds. Immediately repeat the procedure to fashion the remaining cookies. If any of the cookies become hard while they are still on the baking sheet, return them to the oven for a few seconds to soften them.

Shaping Tulipes

1 *SPREADING THE BATTER. Drop a heaping tablespoon of batter onto a prepared baking sheet. With a palette knife or the back of a spoon, spread out the batter in a circular motion to produce disks 6 to 7 inches across. Place two more cookies on the sheet, and bake as directed (right).*

2 *MOLDING THE CUPS. Working rapidly, lift a cookie from the sheet with a metal spatula and place it over the bottom of an overturned drinking glass. Gently press down the cookie's sides with your fingers to form a tulip-like cup. Let the cookie firm up before removing it. Set it aside and proceed to the next tulipe.*

Rolling "Cigarettes"

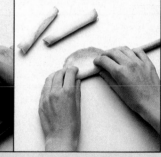

1 *SPREADING THE BATTER. Drop a scant tablespoon of batter onto a prepared baking sheet. With the back of a soup spoon, or a palette knife, spread out the batter in a circular motion, to produce disks 3 to 4 inches across. Repeat the process until the sheet is full, and bake as directed (right).*

2 *ROLLING THE COOKIES. Working rapidly, lift a baked cookie from the sheet with a metal spatula and roll it around a wooden spoon handle or a pencil. When the cookie has firmed up, slide it off and set it aside. Repeat the procedure to form the other cigarettes.*

Stenciling Leaves

1 FILLING THE STENCIL. Place a cookie stencil at the corner of a prepared baking sheet and drop a spoonful of batter into the opening. Holding the stencil steady, use a palette knife or metal spatula to spread the batter in an even layer within the opening. Lift the stencil straight up. Repeat the procedure until cookie leaves fill the baking sheet.

2 DECORATING THE LEAVES. Dip the tip of a small spoon or knife into the chocolate batter prepared according to the recipe (right). Using the spoon or knife like a pen, draw veins on the leaves. Bake and shape the cookies as indicated in the recipe.

Per tulipe:
Calories **68**
Protein **1g.**
Cholesterol **10mg.**
Total fat **4g.**
Saturated fat **2g.**
Sodium **8mg.**

Per leaf:
Calories **51**
Protein **1g.**
Cholesterol **8mg.**
Total fat **3g.**
Saturated fat **2g.**
Sodium **6mg.**

Per cigarette:
Calories **45**
Protein **1g.**
Cholesterol **7mg.**
Total fat **3g.**
Saturated fat **2g.**
Sodium **6mg.**

Shaped Cookies

THIS COOKIE DOUGH CAN BE FASHIONED INTO THE FANCIFUL SHAPES AT LEFT. IT YIELDS ABOUT 12 *TULIPES*, 16 OAK LEAVES OR 18 CIGARETTES.

Working (and total) time: about 40 minutes

4 tbsp. unsalted butter, at room temperature
½ cup confectioners' sugar, sifted
½ tsp. pure vanilla extract
2 tsp. grated grapefruit, orange or lemon zest (optional)
2 egg whites, at room temperature
⅓ cup unbleached all-purpose flour
½ tsp. unsweetened cocoa powder

Lightly oil a baking sheet or line it with parchment paper; preheat the oven to 375° F.

In a large bowl, beat together the butter, sugar, vanilla and the citrus zest, if you are using it. Stir a little of the egg white into the butter mixture. Continue adding the egg white a little at a time, mixing in about 2 tablespoons of the flour after each addition of egg white. Form the batter into one or more of the shapes suggested below.

Tulipes. For each cookie, drop a heaping tablespoon of batter onto the prepared baking sheet and spread as directed in the technique (left). Make no more than three cookies at a time. Bake them until the edges are delicately browned — about five minutes. Shape the cookies as shown in the technique. (If they become too stiff to shape, return them briefly to the oven to soften — about 30 seconds — before continuing.) Repeat the process for the remaining batter. Fill the *tulipes* with ice cream, sorbet or berries just before serving.

Oak leaves. Use an oak-leaf stencil as shown (left) to shape the cookies. Such a stencil can be purchased at cookware stores, or made by tracing an oak leaf on cardboard and cutting out the shape. For the veins, put 1 tablespoon of the batter into a small bowl and sift in the cocoa, then mix the cocoa thoroughly into the batter with a spoon. Use the tip of a small spoon or knife to paint each cookie with veins as directed. Bake the leaves until they are delicately browned at the edges — about five minutes.

Remove the baking sheet and set it on the stove top so it stays warm. Loosen an oak leaf with a metal spatula; working quickly, curl the leaf by bending it over a counter edge. (If the cookies become too stiff to shape, return them briefly to the oven to soften — about 30 seconds — before continuing.) Shape, bake and curl the remaining cookies the same way.

Cigarettes. For each cookie, drop a scant tablespoon of the batter onto a prepared baking sheet and spread it as shown (left). Bake the cookies until the edges are delicately browned — about five minutes. Shape the cigarettes as directed in the technique. (If the cookies become too stiff, return them briefly to the oven to soften — about 30 seconds — before continuing.)

EDITOR'S NOTE: *Store the cookies in an airtight container.*

Fig Bars

Makes about 40 slices
Working time: about 1 hour
Total time: about 3 hours (includes chilling)

Per slice:
Calories **125**
Protein **2g.**
Cholesterol **9mg.**
Total fat **2g.**
Saturated fat **1g.**
Sodium **14mg.**

3 tbsp. unsalted butter
1 tbsp. corn-oil margarine
¾ cup honey
1 egg
grated zest of 1 lemon
½ cup unbleached all-purpose flour
½ tsp. baking powder
2½ cups whole-wheat flour
4 cups dried figs, quartered
½ cup light brown sugar
1 cup unsweetened apple juice

Cream the butter and margarine in a bowl. Beat in the honey, then the egg and lemon zest. Sift the all-purpose flour and baking powder into the bowl; add the whole-wheat flour. Beat the mixture just enough to blend it into a dough. Shape the dough into a disk about 1 inch thick, then encase it in plastic wrap and refrigerate it until it is cold — at least two hours.

While the dough is chilling, make the filling: Put half of the figs, brown sugar and apple juice into a food processor, and finely chop the figs. Scrape the fig mixture into a heavy-bottomed saucepan. Repeat the process with the remaining figs, sugar and juice. Cook the mixture over low heat, stirring occasionally, for 10 minutes. Return the mixture to the food processor and purée it. Transfer the purée to a bowl; cover the bowl and chill it well.

Preheat the oven to 400° F. When the dough is cold, cut it in half. Using a rolling pin, roll out the dough halves on a well-floured work surface to form two 18-by-5-inch rectangles. Divide the filling in half. Roll each piece of filling by hand into a log 17 inches long. Position a filling log lengthwise in the center of each dough rectangle. Fold one long flap of dough over the filling; fold the opposite flap of dough over the first, and press down on the doubled flaps to seal in the filling. Repeat the process to seal in the other log of filling.

Turn the dough rolls seam side down and brush any excess flour off their tops. Pinch closed the two ends of each dough roll. Shape the rolls to make them even and straight, then pat them all over so that the filling adheres to the dough. Place the rolls on a baking sheet; if they do not fit, lay them on the sheet diagonally. Bake them until they are lightly browned — 16 to 18 minutes. Let the rolls cool on the baking sheet for 10 to 15 minutes, then cut each one into ¾-inch-thick slices.

Bananas and Oranges in Chocolate Puffs

Serves 16
Working time: about 45 minutes
Total time: about 1 hour and 45 minutes

Calories **161**
Protein **5g.**
Cholesterol **60mg.**
Total fat **6g.**
Saturated fat **2g.**
Sodium **72mg.**

1 cup unbleached all-purpose flour
1 tbsp. unsweetened cocoa powder
1 tsp. ground cinnamon
½ tsp. grated nutmeg
2 tbsp. unsalted butter
2 tbsp. safflower oil
¼ tsp. salt
2 tbsp. sugar
3 eggs, plus 2 egg whites
4 ripe bananas
4 navel oranges, segmented (technique, page 14)
Ricotta filling
1 cup part-skim ricotta cheese
2 tbsp. sugar
1 tsp. pure vanilla extract
2 tbsp. confectioners' sugar

Mix together the flour, unsweetened cocoa powder, cinnamon and nutmeg; set the mixture aside. Preheat the oven to 400° F.

Combine the butter, oil, salt, sugar and 1 cup of water in a saucepan, and bring the mixture to a boil. As soon as the butter melts, remove the pan from the heat and stir in the flour mixture with a wooden spoon. Return the pan to the stove over medium heat and cook the mixture, stirring vigorously, until it comes cleanly away from the sides of the pan.

Remove the pan from the heat once more and allow it to cool for two minutes before adding the eggs. Incorporate the eggs one at a time, beating vigorously after you add each one, until the dough is smooth. In a separate bowl, whisk the egg whites until they are frothy; beat half of the egg whites into the dough. To test the consistency of the dough, scoop some up with a spoon, then turn the spoon and wait for the dough to fall off; it should fall off cleanly at the count of three. If it does not, beat in more of the egg whites and repeat the test.

Spoon the dough into a pastry bag fitted with a ½-inch star tip. Pipe the dough onto a lightly oiled baking sheet in mounting swirls about 1½ inches across. (If you do not have a pastry bag, fashion 1½-inch mounds with a spoon.) Bake the puffs until they expand and are firm to the touch — about 25 minutes. Turn off the oven, prop the door ajar with a wooden spoon, and let the puffs dry in the oven for 15 minutes. Then transfer them to a rack to cool.

While the puffs are cooling, make the filling: Purée the ricotta in a food processor or a blender, then blend in the sugar and vanilla. Refrigerate the filling.

To assemble the dessert, cut each puff in half horizontally. Fill the lower halves with the chilled ricotta mixture. Peel the bananas and slice them into rounds; then arrange the banana rounds and orange segments on top of the filling. Replace the upper halves of the puffs. Sift the confectioners' sugar over all, and serve the puffs at once.

⅔ cup of the sugar, and the tangerine or orange zest and juice, and mix them thoroughly.

To prepare the meringue, beat the whites and cream of tartar together in another bowl until the whites hold soft peaks. Add the remaining ⅔ cup of sugar 2 tablespoons at a time, beating continuously until the whites are shiny and hold stiff peaks.

Stir one third of the meringue into the cake batter to lighten it, then fold in the remaining meringue. Rinse a 10-inch Bundt cake pan with water and shake it out so that only a few droplets remain. Spoon the batter into the pan and bake the cake for 50 minutes. Increase the oven temperature to 350° F. and continue baking the cake until a tester inserted in the thickest part comes out clean — five to 15 minutes more.

When the cake is done, remove it from the oven and let it rest for 10 minutes. Loosen it from the sides of the pan with a spatula and invert it onto a rack. Allow the cake to cool completely — about one and a half hours.

To prepare the lemon glaze, first sift the confectioners' sugar into a small bowl, then stir in the lemon juice and zest. Continue stirring until a smooth paste results. Stir in the sour cream and pour the glaze over the cake, letting the excess cascade down the sides.

Tangerine Chiffon Cake with Lemon Glaze

Serves 16
Working time: about 30 minutes
Total time: about 3 hours (includes cooling)

Calories **201**
Protein **3g.**
Cholesterol **69mg.**
Total fat **6g.**
Saturated fat **1g.**
Sodium **108mg.**

2 cups cake flour
1 tbsp. baking powder
4 eggs, separated, plus 3 egg whites
⅓ cup safflower oil
1 ⅓ cups sugar
2½ tbsp. finely chopped tangerine zest or grated orange zest
1 cup strained tangerine juice or orange juice, preferably fresh
½ tsp. cream of tartar
Lemon glaze
¾ cup confectioners' sugar
1 tbsp. fresh lemon juice
1 tbsp. grated lemon zest
1 tbsp. sour cream

Preheat the oven to 325° F.

To make the cake batter, sift the flour and baking powder into a large bowl. Whisk in the egg yolks, oil,

Lemon Cornmeal Cake with Blueberry Sauce

Serves 10
Working time: about 35 minutes
Total time: about 1 hour and 30 minutes

Calories **215**
Protein **4g.**
Cholesterol **68mg.**
Total fat **9g.**
Saturated fat **4g.**
Sodium **90mg.**

2 tbsp. sweetened dried coconut
½ cup sugar
¼ cup blanched almonds
1 cup stone-ground yellow cornmeal
½ cup unbleached all-purpose flour
1 ½ tsp. baking powder
½ cup buttermilk
grated zest and juice of 1 lemon
¼ cup unsalted butter
2 eggs
1 pint blueberries
⅛ tsp. ground cinnamon

Preheat the oven to 350° F. Cut pieces of wax paper to fit the bottom and sides of a 9-by-5-inch loaf pan. Line the pan with the wax paper.

Grind the coconut with 1 tablespoon of the sugar in a blender or food processor. Transfer the coconut to a small bowl. Grind the almonds with 1 tablespoon of the remaining sugar in the blender or food processor; transfer the almonds to the bowl containing the coconut, and set it aside.

Sift the cornmeal, flour and baking powder into a bowl. Combine the buttermilk, lemon zest and lemon juice in a measuring cup. Cream the butter and the remaining sugar in a bowl; the mixture should be light and fluffy. Add the eggs one at a time to the creamed butter and sugar, beating well after each addition. Alternately fold in the sifted ingredients and the buttermilk, adding a third of each mixture at a time. When the batter is thoroughly mixed, stir in the ground coconut and almonds.

Spoon the batter into the prepared loaf pan. Bake the cake until a wooden pick inserted in the center comes out clean — 30 to 40 minutes. Cool the pan on a rack for 10 to 15 minutes, then turn out the cake on the rack. Remove the wax paper; set the cake right side up to cool.

Just before serving time, prepare the blueberry sauce. Combine the blueberries and cinnamon in a small, heavy-bottomed saucepan over medium heat. Cook the blueberries, stirring occasionally, until they pop and exude some of their juice — about five minutes. Serve the sauce warm — do not let it cool — with slices of cake.

Glazed Fruit Tartlets

Makes 16 tartlets
Working time: about 1 hour
Total time: about 1 hour and 30 minutes

Per tartlet:
Calories **126**
Protein **2g.**
Cholesterol **4mg.**
Total fat **3g.**
Saturated fat **1g.**
Sodium **70mg.**

1 cup sifted unbleached all-purpose flour
2 tbsp. cold unsalted butter
1 tbsp. corn-oil margarine
½ tsp. salt
2 tbsp. sugar
½ tsp. pure vanilla extract
2 ripe nectarines
1 cup apple jelly
1 cup fresh raspberries
Cream filling
¾ cup low-fat cottage cheese
grated zest of 1 lemon
2 tbsp. sugar

Preheat the oven to 400° F.

To prepare the tartlet dough, put the flour, butter, margarine, salt and the 2 tablespoons of sugar into a food processor or a bowl. Blend the ingredients — using two knives if you are working by hand — just long enough to produce a fine-meal texture. Add the vanilla and 2 tablespoons of water, and continue blending the mixture just until it forms a ball. Shape the dough into a log about 8 inches long, then encase it in plastic wrap, and chill it while you make the cream filling.

For the filling, purée the cottage cheese in the food processor or blender so that the curd is no longer visible, then blend in the lemon zest and the 2 tablespoons of sugar. Refrigerate the filling.

To form the tartlet shells, divide the dough log into 16 equal pieces. Press each piece of dough into a fluted 4-by-2-inch boat-shaped tartlet pan or a fluted 2½-inch round tartlet pan *(technique, page 119)*. Freeze the tartlet shells for 10 minutes. Set the shells on a baking sheet and bake them until their edges start to brown — six to eight minutes. Leave the tartlet shells in their pans to cool to room temperature.

Halve the nectarines lengthwise, discarding the pits, then thinly slice the nectarine halves. Melt the apple jelly in a small saucepan over medium heat, stirring often to prevent sticking. Allow the mixture to cool slightly; it should be thick enough to coat the fruit.

To assemble the desserts, first remove the tartlet shells from the pans, then spread about 2 teaspoons of the chilled filling inside each shell. Arrange the nectarine slices and raspberries atop the filling. Brush the fruit lightly with the warm jelly. If the jelly cools to room temperature, reheat it, stirring constantly, until it is thin enough to spread.

Lining Tartlet Molds with Dough

1 *FILLING THE MOLD. After dividing the dough into 16 equal pieces, as called for in the recipe, press one of the pieces into a tartlet mold and spread it across the bottom with your fingers.*

2 *FORMING THE FLUTED EDGE. Gently force the dough up the fluted sides of the mold, using your fingers; with your thumb, press back down any dough that rises above the top edge of the rim.*

Gingery Peach and Almond Tartlets

Serves 10
Working time: about 45 minutes
Total time: about 1 hour and 30 minutes

Calories **150**
Protein **3g.**
Cholesterol **58mg.**
Total fat **6g.**
Saturated fat **1g.**
Sodium **36mg.**

5 firm but ripe peaches
½ cup blanched almonds
¼ cup unbleached all-purpose flour
½ tsp. baking powder
½ tbsp. finely chopped fresh ginger
½ cup sugar
2 eggs
1 tbsp. unsalted butter, softened

Blanch the peaches in boiling water until their skins loosen — 30 seconds to one minute. Peel the peaches, then cut them in half, discarding the pits.

Preheat the oven to 325° F.

Put the almonds, flour, baking powder, ginger and sugar into a food processor or a blender; blend the mixture until the nuts are very finely chopped. Add the eggs and butter, and process them just long enough to blend them in.

Slice one of the peach halves lengthwise and arrange the slices in a lightly oiled 4-inch tartlet pan. Cut and arrange the remaining peach halves the same way. Spoon the almond mixture over the peaches and bake the tartlets until they are lightly browned — 30 to 40 minutes.

Let the tartlets cool on a wire rack, then remove them from the pans, and serve.

EDITOR'S NOTE: *These tartlets may be made in a muffin pan.*

hands. Encase the dough in plastic wrap and refrigerate it for 20 minutes.

Scatter several tablespoons of cornmeal over a clean work surface and roll out the dough to a thickness of about ⅛ inch. Alternatively, place the dough between two sheets of parchment paper or wax paper, and roll it out. With a cookie cutter, cut the dough into rounds about 4½ inches in diameter. Use the rounds to line eight 3-inch tartlet molds. Chill the molds in the freezer for at least 10 minutes. While the molds are chilling, preheat the oven to 400° F.

Bake the tartlet shells until they have browned and are crisp — 20 to 25 minutes. Remove them from the pans and cool them on a cake rack.

To prepare the tartlet filling, mix together the blueberries, sugar, lemon juice and lemon zest in a saucepan. Bring the mixture to a boil over medium heat, then continue cooking it until the berries have burst and there is about 1 cup of juice in the pan — five to seven minutes. Stir in the tapioca. Cook the filling, stirring frequently, until it boils and thickens slightly — about 10 minutes more. Set the filling aside to cool.

Spoon the cooled filling into the tartlet shells and let them stand for 10 minutes before serving.

Cornmeal Tartlets with Tapioca-Blueberry Filling

Serves 8
Working time: about 20 minutes
Total time: about 1 hour and 20 minutes

Calories **273**
Protein **3g.**
Cholesterol **7mg.**
Total fat **6g.**
Saturated fat **2g.**
Sodium **171mg.**

1 ¼ cups unbleached all-purpose flour
½ cup stone-ground cornmeal
½ cup confectioners' sugar
½ tsp. salt
1 tbsp. cornstarch
2 tbsp. cold unsalted butter, cut into 4 pieces
2 tbsp. cold corn-oil margarine, cut into 4 pieces
Tapioca-blueberry filling
4 cups fresh blueberries, picked over and stemmed, or 4 cups frozen whole blueberries, thawed
½ cup sugar
1 tbsp. fresh lemon juice
2 tsp. grated lemon zest
1 tbsp. tapioca

To prepare the tartlet dough, combine the flour, cornmeal, confectioners' sugar, salt and cornstarch in a food processor or a bowl. If you are using a food processor, add the butter and margarine, and cut them into the dry ingredients with several short bursts. With the motor running, pour in 2 tablespoons of cold water in a thin, steady stream, and blend the dough just until it forms a ball. If the dough is too dry and crumbly, blend in up to 1 tablespoon more of water. If you are making the dough in a bowl, use two knives to cut the butter and margarine into the dry ingredients, then incorporate the water with a wooden spoon or your

Pears with a Spiced Walnut Crust

Serves 10
Working time: about 40 minutes
Total time: about 1 hour and 20 minutes

Calories **285**
Protein **3g.**
Cholesterol **6mg.**
Total fat **9g.**
Saturated fat **2g.**
Sodium **34mg.**

½ cup walnuts (about 2 oz.)
1 cup unbleached all-purpose flour
⅓ cup light brown sugar
2 tbsp. unsalted butter
2 tbsp. corn-oil margarine
¼ tsp. ground mace
¼ tsp. ground ginger
grated zest of 1 lemon
½ tsp. pure vanilla extract
6 pears
1 cup apple jelly

Preheat the oven to 375° F.

Spread the walnuts on a baking sheet and toast them in the oven until their skins begin to pull away — about 10 minutes. Then allow the walnuts cool to room temperature.

Put the toasted walnuts, flour, brown sugar, butter, margarine, mace, ginger and lemon zest into a food processor. Process the mixture until it resembles coarse meal. Sprinkle the vanilla and 1 tablespoon of water over the mixture, and process it in short bursts just until it begins to hold together in dough pieces about 1 inch in diameter. (Do not overprocess the dough lest it form a ball.)

Transfer the pieces of dough to a clean work surface. Rub the pieces between your fingers to finish blending the dough, then put the pieces into a 9-inch tart pan with a removable bottom. Spread out the dough with your fingers, coating the bottom and sides of the pan with a very thin layer; crimp the top edge of the dough with your fingers. Put the pan into the refrigerator.

Peel, halve, and core the pears. Thinly slice each pear half crosswise, then arrange 10 of the pear halves around the edge of the tart shell, pointing their narrow ends toward the center. Flatten each half, slightly spreading out the slices. Arrange the two remaining halves in the center of the tart.

Bake the tart until the edges are browned and any juices rendered by the pears have evaporated — about 40 minutes. Set the tart aside to cool.

Cook the apple jelly in a small saucepan over medium-low heat until it melts — about four minutes. Using a pastry brush, glaze the cooled pears with a thin coating of the melted jelly.

EDITOR'S NOTE: *If you do not have a food processor, grind the walnuts in a blender together with 1 tablespoon of sugar, then prepare the dough in a bowl with a pastry blender and a wooden spoon.*

Crepes with Glazed Pears

Serves 4
Working time: about 1 hour
Total time: about 3 hours

Calories **304**
Protein **5g.**
Cholesterol **79mg.**
Total fat **11g.**
Saturated fat **3g.**
Sodium **71mg.**

3 ripe pears
1 tbsp. fresh lemon juice
½ tsp. safflower oil
¼ cup Sauternes or other sweet white wine
3 tbsp. honey
1 tbsp. unsalted butter
freshly ground black pepper
Sauternes crepe batter
¼ cup plus 3 tbsp. unbleached all-purpose flour
1/16 tsp. salt
freshly ground black pepper
⅛ tsp. sugar
1 egg
2 tbsp. Sauternes or other sweet white wine
1½ tbsp. safflower oil
½ to ¾ cup low-fat milk

To prepare the crepe batter, whisk together the flour, salt, some pepper, the sugar, egg, wine, oil and ½ cup of the milk in a bowl. Whisking constantly, pour in enough additional milk in a fine, steady stream to thin the batter to the consistency of heavy cream. Cover the bowl and refrigerate it for at least two hours.

Peel, core and slice the pears. Sprinkle the slices with the lemon juice and set them aside while you cook the crepes.

Heat a crepe pan or an 8-inch nonstick skillet over medium-high heat. Pour in the ½ teaspoon of oil and spread it over the entire surface with a paper towel. Pour 2 to 3 tablespoons of the batter into the hot pan and swirl the pan just enough to coat the bottom with a thin, even layer of batter. Pour any excess batter back into the bowl. Cook the crepe until the bottom is brown — about 30 seconds — then lift the edge of the crepe and turn it over. Cook the second side until it is brown — about 15 seconds more — and slide the crepe onto a plate. The crepe should be paper-thin; if it is not, stir a bit more milk into the batter. Repeat the process with the remaining batter to form eight crepes in all. If you are using a crepe pan, you may have to oil it again to prevent sticking.

Fold a crepe in half, then in thirds. Repeat the process to fold the remaining crepes. Put two on each of four dessert plates, and set them aside in a warm place.

Bring the wine and honey to a boil in a skillet over medium-high heat. Cook the mixture until it is syrupy — about two minutes. Add the butter and the pears, and continue cooking the mixture until the pears are barely tender and have become glazed with the mixture — about three minutes more.

With a slotted spoon, remove the pears from the skillet and divide them evenly among the four plates. Pour a little of the syrup remaining in the skillet over each portion; grind a generous amount of black pepper over all and serve at once.

Fruit-and-Nut-Filled Phyllo Roll

Serves 6
Working time: about 40 minutes
Total time: about 1 hour and 10 minutes

Calories **186**
Protein **4g.**
Cholesterol **8mg.**
Total fat **6g.**
Saturated fat **2g.**
Sodium **2mg.**

1 egg white
¼ cup part-skim ricotta cheese
1 orange
1 tsp. grated lemon zest
¼ tsp. ground cinnamon
⅛ tsp. grated nutmeg
⅛ tsp. ground allspice
⅛ tsp. salt
3 tbsp. coarsely chopped pecans
½ cup raisins
1 tbsp. pure maple syrup
¼ cup sugar
2 slices whole-wheat bread, toasted
2 sheets frozen phyllo dough, thawed
1 tbsp. unsalted butter, melted

To make the filling, first mix together the egg white and the ricotta. With a vegetable peeler or a paring knife, remove the zest from the orange and reserve it. Cut away all the white pith and discard it. Working over a bowl to catch the juice, segment the orange as shown on page 14, dropping the segments into the bowl. Squeeze the last drops of juice from the pulpy core of membranes into the bowl. Coarsely chop the orange zest and orange segments, and add them to the ricotta mixture along with the juice that has collected in the bowl. Stir in the lemon zest, cinnamon, nutmeg, allspice, salt, pecans, raisins, maple syrup and sugar. Cut the toasted bread slices into cubes and mix them into the filling. Set the filling aside.

Preheat the oven to 350° F.

Lay one of the phyllo sheets on a piece of wax paper that is slightly larger than the phyllo. Lightly brush the phyllo with some of the butter. Set the second sheet of phyllo squarely atop the first.

Spoon the filling down one of the longer sides of the doubled phyllo sheet, leaving about 1½ inches uncovered at both ends of the filling. To avoid tearing the phyllo, lift the edge of the wax paper and roll the phyllo once around the filling. Continue rolling the phyllo and filling away from you to form a compact cylinder. Tuck under the two open ends of the roll and transfer it to a lightly oiled baking sheet. Brush the top of the roll with the remaining butter and bake it until it is golden brown — about 30 minutes. Allow the roll to cool, then slice it into serving rounds.

the meringues stand at room temperature until they cool — they will become quite crisp.

Purée the ricotta with the yogurt in a food processor or a blender. Divide the cheese mixture among the meringue baskets, and top each with some of the strawberries and blueberries.

Berry-Filled Meringue Baskets

Serves 8
Working time: about 50 minutes
Total time: about 5 hours (includes drying)

Calories **150**
Protein **4g.**
Cholesterol **5mg.**
Total fat **2g.**
Saturated fat **1g.**
Sodium **45mg.**

3 egg whites
1 cup sugar
½ cup part-skim ricotta cheese
¼ cup plain low-fat yogurt
2 cups hulled, sliced strawberries
1 cup blueberries, stemmed, picked over and rinsed

Line a baking sheet with parchment paper or with a paper bag that has been cut open and flattened. Preheat the oven to 160° F. If your oven does not have a setting this low, set it just below 200° F. Keep the oven door propped open with a ball of crumpled foil.

To prepare the meringue, put the egg whites and sugar into a large, heatproof bowl. Set the bowl over a pan of simmering water, and stir the mixture with a whisk until the sugar has dissolved and the egg whites are hot — about six minutes. Remove the bowl from the heat. Using an electric mixer, beat the egg whites on medium-high speed until they form stiff peaks and have cooled to room temperature.

Transfer the meringue to a pastry bag fitted with a ½-inch star tip. Holding the tip about ½ inch above the surface of the baking sheet, pipe out the meringue in a tightly coiled spiral until you have formed a flat disk about 3½ inches across. Pipe a single ring of meringue on top of the edge of the disk, forming a low wall that will hold in the filling. Form seven more meringue baskets the same way.

Put the baking sheet into the oven and let the meringues bake for at least four hours. The meringues should remain white and be thoroughly dried out. Let

Rolled Cherry-Walnut Cake

Serves 8
Working time: about 1 hour
Total time: about 1 hour and 30 minutes

Calories **142**
Protein **5g.**
Cholesterol **70mg.**
Total fat **4g.**
Saturated fat **1g.**
Sodium **72mg.**

¼ cup walnuts, finely chopped
1½ tbsp. unbleached all-purpose flour
½ tsp. baking powder
2 eggs, separated, plus 1 egg white, the whites at room temperature
2 tbsp. dark brown sugar
½ tsp. pure vanilla extract
¼ cup sugar
2 tsp. confectioners' sugar
Cherry filling
½ tsp. pure vanilla extract
1 cup plain low-fat yogurt
2 tbsp. sugar
½ lb. fresh cherries, pitted (technique, page 24) and quartered

Dot the corners and center of a baking sheet with butter. Line the sheet with parchment paper or wax paper — the butter will hold the paper in place. Lightly butter the top of the paper, then dust it with flour and set the pan aside. Heat the oven to 350° F.

Mix together the walnuts, flour and baking powder in a small bowl; set the mixture aside.

Beat the two egg yolks with the brown sugar and 1½ tablespoons of very hot water until the mixture is thick enough to fall in a ribbon when the beater is lifted from the bowl — about four minutes. Stir in the vanilla and set the bowl aside.

Beat the three egg whites on medium speed in a bowl until they form soft peaks. Increase the speed to medium high and continue beating, gradually adding the ¼ cup of sugar, until stiff peaks form.

Stir about one fourth of the egg whites into the yolk mixture to lighten it. Gently fold one third of the remaining egg whites into the yolk mixture, then fold in half of the nut-and-flour mixture, followed by half of the remaining egg whites. Finally, fold in the remaining nut-and-flour mixture and the last of the egg whites.

Transfer the batter to the baking sheet and spread it

out, forming a rectangle about 11 by 7 inches. Bake the cake until it is lightly browned and springy to the touch — about 20 minutes. Let the cake cool completely — at least 30 minutes.

Sprinkle a sheet of parchment paper or wax paper with confectioners' sugar and invert the cake onto the paper. Gently remove the paper on which the cake baked from the bottom of the cake. Trim the edges of

the cake with a serrated knife or scissors. Stir the vanilla into the yogurt, then spread this mixture onto the cake, leaving a ½-inch border uncovered all around. Sprinkle the sugar over the yogurt mixture, then scatter the cherries evenly on top. Starting at a long side, roll the cake into a cylinder. Set the cake on a platter; sprinkle the confectioners' sugar over the top just before serving.

5 *Sugar-topped chocolate squares, flavored with bourbon, took just eight minutes to bake in the microwave oven (recipe, right).*

Desserts from the Microwave

Custards, puddings and fruits may seem unlikely candidates for the microwave oven, but they are only a few of the many desserts that are perfectly suited to the microwave process. When prepared conventionally, puddings and some custards require constant stirring to keep the mixture smooth and prevent it from burning. In the microwave they need be stirred only occasionally (the maple custard on page 135 is not stirred at all), and there is no danger of scorching them.

Because of their high juice content, fruits that are baked in a microwave require little added liquid — and, since they cook quickly, they lose few of their water-soluble vitamins. Fruits retain their shape, texture and much of their inviting color as well. One caution: Avoid microwaving overripe fruits — they may soften to the point of disintegrating.

Since some cakes and cookies fail to brown in the microwave, they are not suitable for the process. Still, bar cookies and cakes that have color in themselves, such as those made with chocolate, or those with fruit at the bottom, fare very well indeed, as evidenced by the Bourbon Chocolate Squares on page 127 or the Rhubarb-Gingerbread Cake on page 136.

The microwave oven offers another boon to cooks. It can abbreviate the time normally required for many of the simple chores associated with dessert preparation. Not only does the microwave dispense with the double boiler used for melting chocolate, but it can melt an ounce of chocolate in just one and a half to two minutes — less than one third the customary time. Similarly, hard fruit, requiring long baking in a conventional oven, softens in the microwave in minutes.

Although power settings often vary among different manufacturers' ovens, the recipes use "high" to indicate 100 percent power, "medium high" for 70 percent, "medium" for 50 percent and "medium low" for 30 percent. All custards, puddings and fruits are microwaved on high.

Bourbon Chocolate Squares

Makes 20 squares
Working time: about 40 minutes
Total time: about 2 hours

Per square:
Calories **92**
Protein **1g.**
Cholesterol **33mg.**
Total fat **4g.**
Saturated fat **2g.**
Sodium **45mg.**

2 eggs, separated
¾ cup plus 2 tbsp. sugar
1½ tsp. pure vanilla extract
2 tbsp. bourbon
½ tbsp. fresh lemon juice
1 cup cake flour
½ tsp. baking powder
¼ tsp. salt
1½ oz. unsweetened chocolate
3½ tbsp. unsalted butter

Whisk together the egg yolks, ½ cup of the sugar and 1 tablespoon of hot water until the mixture is light and frothy — about five minutes. Whisk in the vanilla, bourbon and lemon juice.

Sift the flour, baking powder and salt over the egg-yolk mixture. Gently fold the two together, then set the batter aside.

Put the chocolate and butter into a small dish. Microwave them on high for two minutes. (Although the chocolate will appear not to have melted, it will nonetheless be soft.) Stir the chocolate and butter together, then fold them into the batter.

Beat the egg whites until they form soft peaks. Continue beating the whites, gradually adding ¼ cup of the remaining sugar, until the whites form stiff peaks.

Fold the beaten whites into the batter and spoon the batter into a lightly oiled 8-inch-square baking dish. Microwave the dish on medium (50 percent power) for 8 minutes, rotating the dish a quarter turn every two minutes.

Remove the dish from the oven and sprinkle the remaining 2 tablespoons of sugar over the top. Let the cake stand at room temperature until it is cool — about one hour. Cut the cake into 20 squares and serve.

EDITOR'S NOTE: *These squares taste even better when refrigerated for 24 hours.*

Fresh Blueberries with a Dumpling Topping

Serves 4
Working time: about 30 minutes
Total time: about 40 minutes

Calories **293**
Protein **4g.**
Cholesterol **10mg.**
Total fat **4g.**
Saturated fat **2g.**
Sodium **244mg.**

3 cups fresh blueberries, picked over and stemmed
½ cup sugar
¼ tsp. ground cinnamon
⅛ tsp. grated nutmeg
½ tbsp. fresh lemon juice
Dumpling topping
¾ cup unbleached all-purpose flour
1 tbsp. sugar
½ tbsp. baking powder
⅛ tsp. salt
grated zest of ½ lemon
1 tbsp. cold unsalted butter
½ cup low-fat milk

Mix the blueberries, sugar, cinnamon, nutmeg and lemon juice in a 1 ½-quart soufflé dish or baking dish. Cover the dish with plastic wrap and microwave it on high for two minutes. Set the dish aside, still covered.

For the topping, combine the flour, sugar, baking powder, salt and lemon zest in a food processor. Cut the butter into the dry ingredients, then blend in the milk. (Alternatively, prepare the topping in a bowl, cutting the butter into the dry ingredients with a pastry cutter and blending in the milk with a wooden spoon.) Stop mixing the topping as soon as the milk is incorporated.

Drop the topping onto the blueberries in four rounded tablespoonfuls. Microwave the blueberries, uncovered, on medium (50 percent power) for six minutes, turning the dish after three minutes. Let the dessert stand for two minutes before serving.

Chocolate Pudding Cake

Serves 10
Working time: about 20 minutes
Total time: about 40 minutes

Calories **191**
Protein **3g.**
Cholesterol **1mg.**
Total fat **5g.**
Saturated fat **1g.**
Sodium **150mg.**

½ cup plus ⅓ cup sugar
1 cup cake flour
¼ tsp. salt
6 tbsp. unsweetened cocoa powder
2 tsp. baking powder
½ cup low-fat milk
2 tbsp. safflower oil
1 ½ tsp. pure vanilla extract
¼ cup chopped walnuts (about 1 oz.)
⅓ cup light brown sugar
1 tbsp. confectioners' sugar

Lightly butter a 9-inch pie pan and dust it with unsweetened cocoa powder.

In a bowl, sift together ½ cup of the sugar, the cake flour, salt, 3 tablespoons of the cocoa powder and the baking powder. Add the milk, oil and 1 teaspoon of the vanilla, then stir to combine the liquid ingredients with the dry. Stir in the walnuts, and spread the cake batter evenly in the pie pan.

Mix together the remaining ⅓ cup of sugar, the remaining 3 tablespoons of cocoa powder and the brown sugar. Stir in the remaining ½ teaspoon of vanilla and 1 cup of water. Pour this liquid over the batter in the pie pan.

Microwave the cake on medium (50 percent power) for 18 to 20 minutes, rotating the dish a quarter turn every three minutes. Serve the cake warm. Just before serving, sift the confectioners' sugar onto the cake.

Vanilla Custard with Yogurt and Apricots

Serves 10
Working time: about 30 minutes
Total time: about 1 hour and 30 minutes
(includes chilling)

Calories **207**
Protein **6g.**
Cholesterol **63mg.**
Total fat **3g.**
Saturated fat **2g.**
Sodium **112mg.**

¼ lb. dried apricots, coarsely chopped
1 cup plus 1 tbsp. sugar
⅓ cup cornstarch
⅛ tsp. salt
4 cups low-fat milk
one 2-inch length of vanilla bean, split lengthwise, or 1 tsp. pure vanilla extract
2 eggs, beaten
¾ cup plain low-fat yogurt

Combine the apricots with ½ cup of water and 1 tablespoon of the sugar in a glass bowl. Cover the bowl with plastic wrap and microwave the mixture on high, stopping midway to stir it, until the apricots are tender — four to six minutes. Purée the mixture in a food processor or a blender, then return the purée to the bowl. Cover the bowl and refrigerate it.

Combine the cornstarch, salt and the remaining cup of sugar in a small bowl. Pour the milk into a 2-quart glass bowl and add the cornstarch mixture. Whisk the mixture until the cornstarch is completely dissolved. Add the vanilla bean, if you are using it. Microwave the mixture on high, stopping once or twice to stir it, until the milk is hot — about eight minutes.

If you are using the vanilla bean, remove it from the milk and scrape the seeds inside it into the milk. Discard the bean.

Whisk about ½ cup of the hot milk into the eggs. Immediately whisk the egg-milk mixture — and the vanilla extract, if you are using it — into the remaining hot milk. Microwave the mixture on high for three minutes. Whisk the mixture and continue cooking it on high, whisking every 60 seconds, until it thickens — two to three minutes more. Divide the custard among 10 dessert cups and put them into the refrigerator for at least one hour.

Just before serving, spread a dollop of yogurt over each custard and top it with the apricot purée.

EDITOR'S NOTE: *This custard may be prepared up to 24 hours before it is served.*

Baked Apples Filled with Cranberries and Golden Raisins

Serves 6
Working time: about 20 minutes
Total time: about 40 minutes

Calories **209**
Protein **1g.**
Cholesterol **8mg.**
Total fat **4g.**
Saturated fat **2g.**
Sodium **8mg.**

2½ cups fresh or frozen cranberries
½ cup light brown sugar
3 tbsp. golden raisins, chopped
1½ tbsp. unsalted butter
6 Golden Delicious apples

Put the cranberries into a glass bowl and sprinkle the brown sugar over them. Cover the bowl with plastic wrap and microwave the berries on high for two minutes. Stir in the raisins and 1 tablespoon of the butter, re-cover the bowl, and cook the mixture on high until the berries start to burst — one and a half to two and a half minutes. Stir the mixture well and set it aside.

Core one of the apples with a melon baller or a small spoon, scooping out the center of the apple to form a conical cavity about 1¼ inches wide at the top and only ½ inch wide at the bottom. Using a channel knife or a paring knife, cut two grooves for decoration around the apple. Prepare the other apples the same way.

Fill the apples with the cranberry mixture. Arrange the apples in a ring around the edge of a glass pie plate

and dot them with the remaining ½ tablespoon of butter. Cover the filled apples with wax paper and microwave them on high for five minutes. Rotate the plate and each apple 180 degrees, and cook the apples on high for three to five minutes more. Let the apples stand for about five minutes before serving them with their baking juices ladled over the top.

Coffee Soufflé

Serves 8
Working time: about 15 minutes
Total time: about 25 minutes

Calories **101**
Protein **4g.**
Cholesterol **5mg.**
Total fat **2g.**
Saturated fat **1g.**
Sodium **59mg.**

½ cup sugar
1 tbsp. unsalted butter
3 tbsp. unbleached all-purpose flour
2 tsp. instant coffee, mixed with 2 tbsp. boiling water
2 tbsp. Cointreau or other orange-flavored liqueur (optional)
1 tsp. pure vanilla extract
¾ cup evaporated milk
5 egg whites, at room temperature
chocolate mocha-bean candies (optional)

Lightly butter the inside of a 5-cup soufflé mold. Put about 2 teaspoons of the sugar into the mold, then rotate the mold, tilting it in all directions to coat its sides and bottom. Refrigerate the mold.

Put the tablespoon of butter into a 2-quart glass bowl. Microwave it on high until the butter melts — about 45 seconds. Whisk the flour into the butter to form a smooth paste. Add the coffee, the liqueur if you are using it, and the vanilla. Whisk the coffee base until it is smooth again, then stir in the evaporated milk, and microwave it on high for one and a half minutes. Stir the coffee base; microwave it on high until it has thickened — about one minute more. Whisk the coffee base once more, then add all but 2 tablespoons of the remaining sugar. Mix thoroughly and set the bowl aside.

In a separate bowl, beat the egg whites until they form soft peaks. Add the remaining 2 tablespoons of sugar a little at a time, beating continuously until the whites are shiny and hold stiff peaks.

Stir one fourth of the whites into the coffee base to lighten it. Gently — but quickly — fold the coffee base into the remaining whites. Spoon the mixture into the buttered mold, then microwave it on medium low (30 percent power) for 10 to 12 minutes, rotating the mold a quarter turn every three minutes. The soufflé should rise about one inch above the rim of the mold and appear set. Serve the soufflé immediately, garnished, if you like, with the mocha-bean candies.

Mocha Pudding

Serves 6
Working time: about 20 minutes
Total time: about 1 hour and 20 minutes
(includes chilling)

Calories **219**
Protein **5g.**
Cholesterol **11mg.**
Total fat **7g.**
Saturated fat **4g.**
Sodium **108mg.**

1½ oz. unsweetened chocolate
2½ cups low-fat milk
½ cup double-strength coffee
¼ cup cornstarch
¾ cup sugar
⅛ tsp. salt
3 tbsp. half-and-half

Place the chocolate in a 2-quart glass bowl and cook it on medium (50 percent power) for two to three minutes. (Though the chocolate will appear not to have melted, it will be soft.) Whisk the milk and coffee into the chocolate. Combine the cornstarch, sugar and salt, and whisk them into the milk mixture. Microwave the contents of the bowl on high for four minutes. Whisk the mixture and continue cooking it on high, whisking every 60 seconds, until it thickens — four to six minutes more. Pour the pudding into six dessert cups and refrigerate them for at least one hour.

Just before serving the pudding, dribble ½ tablespoon of the half-and-half over each portion.

Tapioca-Rum Pudding with Orange

Serves 6
Working time: about 30 minutes
Total time: about 1 hour and 30 minutes
(includes chilling)

Calories **153**
Protein **5g.**
Cholesterol **52mg.**
Total fat **3g.**
Saturated fat **1g.**
Sodium **104mg.**

1 egg, separated, the white at room temperature	
2 cups low-fat milk	
2 tbsp. white rum	
¼ cup instant tapioca	
5 tbsp. sugar	
1 tsp. grated orange zest	
⅛ tsp. salt	
2 navel oranges	

Whisk together the egg yolk, milk and rum in a 2-quart glass bowl. Stir in the tapioca, 3 tablespoons of the sugar, the orange zest and the salt, and allow the mix-ture to stand for five minutes to soften the tapioca.

Microwave the mixture on high, stopping three or four times to whisk it, until it thickens — six to eight minutes. Remove the bowl from the oven and set it aside while you prepare the meringue.

In a bowl, beat the egg white until soft peaks form. Beating continuously, gradually add the remaining 2 tablespoons of sugar; continue beating the meringue until it forms stiff peaks.

Mix about one third of the meringue into the tapioca mixture to lighten it, then gently fold in the remaining meringue. Spoon the pudding into six dessert cups and refrigerate them until the dessert has cooled — ap-proximately one hour.

While the pudding cools, peel and segment the or-anges *(technique, page 14)*. Garnish each pudding with a few orange segments just before serving.

Maple Custard
with Walnuts

Serves 4
Working time: about 15 minutes
Total time: about 1 hour (includes cooling)

Calories **154**
Protein **7g.**
Cholesterol **76mg.**
Total fat **4g.**
Saturated fat **2g.**
Sodium **99mg.**

1 egg, plus 2 egg whites
⅓ cup maple syrup
1 tsp. pure vanilla extract
1½ cups low-fat milk
4 walnut halves

In a large bowl, whisk together the egg, egg whites, maple syrup and vanilla extract. Pour in the milk and continue whisking the mixture until the eggs are completely blended in.

Pour the mixture into four 4-ounce baking dishes or ramekins. Microwave the custards on medium (50 percent power), rearranging the dishes every three minutes, just until the custards set — about seven minutes in all. Allow the custards to cool to room temperature before transferring them to the refrigerator.

Serve the custards still in their dishes or unmold them first. Present each one with a walnut half on top.

Place a flat, straight-edged object — a spatula, for example, or a piece of cardboard — over one half of a toast triangle and use a sieve to dust the exposed portion with some of the confectioners' sugar. Repeat the process to dust the remaining toast triangles, and serve them alongside the rhubarb applesauce.

Rhubarb Applesauce with Sugar Toast

Serves 6
Working time: about 25 minutes
Total time: about 40 minutes

Calories **206**
Protein **2g.**
Cholesterol **5mg.**
Total fat **3g.**
Saturated fat **1g.**
Sodium **61mg.**

1 ½ lb. tart green apples, preferably Granny Smith, peeled, cored and coarsely chopped
1 tbsp. fresh lemon juice
½ lb. fresh rhubarb, finely chopped, or ½ lb. frozen rhubarb, thawed and finely chopped
½ cup sugar
¼ cup dry sherry
⅛ tsp. grated nutmeg
3 slices white bread, crusts removed
1 tbsp. unsalted butter
2 tbsp. confectioners' sugar

Toss the chopped apple with the lemon juice in a 2-quart baking dish. Add the rhubarb, sugar, sherry and nutmeg. Cover the dish and microwave it on high for 10 to 12 minutes, stirring the mixture every three minutes. The rhubarb and apples should be very tender.

Meanwhile, to make the sugar toast, cut each slice of bread diagonally into two triangles. Melt the butter in a heavy-bottomed skillet over medium heat. Lightly brush both sides of each bread triangle with the butter. Return the triangles to the skillet and cook them until they have browned. Transfer the toast to a rack to cool.

Rhubarb-Gingerbread Upside-Down Cake

Serves 8
Working time: about 20 minutes
Total time: about 50 minutes

Calories **200**
Protein **4g.**
Cholesterol **42mg.**
Total fat **4g.**
Saturated fat **2g.**
Sodium **202mg.**

2 tbsp. unsalted butter
⅓ cup light brown sugar
2 cups coarsely chopped fresh rhubarb or coarsely chopped frozen rhubarb, thawed
1 cup unbleached all-purpose flour
½ cup whole-wheat flour
1 tsp. baking soda
1 tsp. ground ginger
1 tsp. ground cinnamon
½ tsp. grated nutmeg
¼ tsp. dry mustard
¼ tsp. ground cloves
¼ tsp. salt
1 egg
½ cup dark molasses
1 tsp. pure vanilla extract

Put the butter into a 9-inch glass pie plate and microwave it on high for 45 seconds. Smear the butter over the bottom of the plate, coating it evenly, then sprinkle in the brown sugar. Scatter the rhubarb over the sugar.

In a large bowl, combine the all-purpose flour, whole-wheat flour, baking soda, ginger, cinnamon, nutmeg, mustard, cloves and salt. In a second bowl, mix the egg, molasses, vanilla and ½ cup of hot water.

Stir the liquid into the dry ingredients, forming a smooth batter. Pour the batter into the pie plate and microwave it on high for 10 minutes, turning the dish every three minutes.

Remove the cake from the oven and let it stand for five minutes. Run the tip of a knife around the sides of the cake. Invert a serving plate on top of the pie plate and turn both over together; do not remove the pie plate. Let the cake stand for five minutes more, then lift away the pie plate. The cake is best served warm.

EDITOR'S NOTE: *This cake is an ideal showcase for other fruits as well. Two cups of coarsely chopped plums, sour cherries or peeled pears might be substituted for the rhubarb.*

Glossary

Almond paste: a mixture of ground almonds and sugar, used in making pastry fillings and toppings as well as cookies and candies.

Amaretto: an almond-flavored liqueur.

Armagnac: a dry brandy, often more strongly flavored than Cognac, from the Armagnac district of southwest France.

Arrowroot: a tasteless, starchy, white powder refined from the root of a tropical plant; it is used to thicken puddings and sauces. Unlike flour, it is transparent when cooked.

Baking powder: a leavening agent that releases carbon dioxide during baking, causing cake or cookie batter to rise.

Balsamic vinegar: a mildly acid, intensely fragrant wine-based vinegar made in Modena, Italy. Traditionally it is aged in wooden casks.

Bavarian: classically, a cold, rich, gelled dessert made with custard and whipped cream. The lighter version in this book uses Italian meringue and yogurt.

Bombe: a hemispherical mold used for preparing a frozen dessert with several layers of different flavors and colors. Also the contents of such a mold.

Brûlée: a French adjective based on the verb "bruler," (to burn); used to describe the caramelized topping on a dessert.

Bundt pan: a decoratively fluted tube-cake pan. The tube conducts heat into the center of the batter, ensuring even cooking.

Buttermilk: a tangy, cultured-milk product that, despite its name, contains about one third less fat than whole milk.

Calorie (kilocalorie): a unit of measurement used to gauge the amount of energy a food supplies when it is broken down for use in the body.

Cappuccino: espresso mixed with hot frothed milk or cream, and a flavoring, usually cinnamon.

Caramelize: to heat sugar, or a naturally sugar-rich food such as fruit, until it becomes brown and syrupy.

Cardamom: the bittersweet dried seeds of a plant in the ginger family. Cardamom may be used either whole or ground.

Cassis: a liqueur made from black currants.

Cholesterol: a waxlike substance manufactured in the human liver, and also found in foods of animal origin. Although a certain amount of cholesterol is necessary for producing hormones and building cell walls, an excess can accumulate in the arteries, contributing to heart disease. See also Monounsaturated fat; Polyunsaturated fat; Saturated fat.

Chou-puff dough (also called cream-puff dough): a pastry dough, made from water or milk, butter, flour, and eggs, that puffs up in the oven when it is baked. The recipes for chou-puff dough in this book replace some of the egg yolk traditionally called for with egg white and use safflower oil instead of butter to reduce cholesterol.

Cream-puff dough: see Chou-puff dough.

Churn-freezing: preparing a frozen dessert by stirring it continuously with a paddle during the freezing process.

Cobbler: a moist, deep-dish fruit dessert that resembles a pie but lacks a bottom crust. In traditional cobblers, the crust consists of biscuit dough.

Cocoa powder: the result of pulverizing roasted cocoa beans, then removing most of the fat, or cocoa butter.

Confectioners' sugar (also called powdered sugar or 10X sugar — its most refined form): finely ground granulated sugar, with a small amount of added cornstarch to ensure a powdery consistency. The sugar's ability to dissolve instantly makes it ideal for desserts in which a grainy texture is undesirable.

Cornstarch: a starchy white powder made from corn kernels and used to thicken many puddings and sauces. Like arrowroot, it is transparent when cooked and makes a more efficient thickener than flour. When cooked conventionally, a liquid containing cornstarch must be stirred constantly in the early stages to prevent lumps from forming.

Cream of tartar: a natural, mild acid in powder form with a slightly sour taste, used to stabilize beaten egg whites. It should be used sparingly — no more than 1/8 teaspoon to one egg white. Beating egg whites in a copper bowl has a similar stabilizing effect.

Crepe: a paper-thin pancake that can accommodate a variety of fillings, among them fruit purées and poached fruit. Often served with a sauce or a wine- or spirit-based syrup.

Crisp: a dessert of cooked fruit with a crumbly topping that is baked to make it crisp.

Crystallized ginger (also called candied ginger): the spicy, rootlike stems of ginger preserved with sugar. Crystallized ginger should not be confused with ginger in syrup.

Espresso: very strong coffee made by forcing a combination of steam and water through an especially dark and powdery grind of coffee beans.

Fat: a basic component of many foods, comprising three types of fatty acid — saturated, monounsaturated and polyunsaturated — in varying proportions. See also Monounsaturated fat; Polyunsaturated fat; Saturated fat.

Filbert (also called hazelnut): the fruit of a shrublike tree found primarily in Turkey, Italy and Spain, and in the states of Washington and Oregon. Filberts, which are cultivated, have a stronger flavor than hazelnuts, which grow wild. Both are prized by bakers and candymakers.

Gelatin: a virtually tasteless protein, available in powdered form or in sheets. Dissolved gelatin is used to gel chilled desserts so that they retain their shape when unmolded.

Gewürztraminer (also called Traminer): a flowery white wine with a particular affinity for fruit.

Ginger: the spicy, buff-colored rhizome, or rootlike stem, of the ginger plant, used as a seasoning either in fresh form or dried and powdered. See also Crystallized ginger.

Glaze: to coat the surface of a tart or cake with a thin, shiny layer of melted jam or caramel.

Grand Marnier: a high-quality liqueur made from Cognac and orange peel, with a distinctive orange flavor.

Green peppercorns: the small, round, unripened berries of the pepper vine, preserved in water or vinegar. Their taste is less pronounced than that of dried black or white peppercorns.

Grenadine: a sweet, deep red syrup made from pomegranates and sugar; used as a coloring as well as a flavoring in cold desserts and in drinks.

Hazelnut: see Filbert.

Italian meringue: a type of meringue created by beating together hot sugar syrup and egg whites. Italian meringue is used in this book as the basis for mousses, parfaits and cheesecakes, and as a substitute for whipped cream. See also Meringue.

Jalapeño chili pepper: a squat, green, hot chili pepper. It should be handled with the utmost care, for its volatile oils can irritate the skin and burn the eyes.

Julienne: to slice a food into matchstick-size pieces; also, the name for the pieces themselves.

Kirsch (also called Kirschwasser): a clear cherry brandy distilled from small black cherries grown in Switzerland, Germany and the Alsace region of France; often used to macerate fruit desserts.

Kiwi fruit: an egg-shaped fruit with a fuzzy brown skin, tart, lime green flesh and hundreds of tiny black edible seeds. Peeled and sliced, the kiwi displays a starburst of seeds at its center that lends a decorative note to tarts and other desserts.

Kugel: a noodle pudding cooked in a casserole or a skillet.

Mace: the pulverized covering of the nutmeg seed, widely used as a flavoring agent in baking.

Macerate: to soak a food — usually fruit — in sweetened lemon juice, wine or liqueur until the food softens and absorbs the flavors of the liquid.

Madeleine tray: a specialized mold with scallop-shaped indentations, designed for making small cakes but used in this book for molding sorbet.

Mango: a fruit grown throughout the tropics, with sweet, succulent, yellow-orange flesh that is extremely rich in vitamin A. Like papaya, it may cause an allergic reaction in some individuals.

Melon baller: a kitchen tool with a sharp-edged, stainless-steel scoop at each end; it is used to cut perfect spheres of flesh from melons and other fruits.

Meringue: an airy concoction made from stiffly beaten egg whites and sugar. It serves as the base for mousses and soufflés and is folded into angel food and chiffon cake batters. Meringue may also be baked to produce edible baskets for ice cream or other frozen fillings. See also Italian meringue.

Mocha: a flavoring made by combining chocolate and coffee.

Monounsaturated fat: one of three types of fatty acid found in fats. Recent research has shown that some monounsaturated fats may lower blood cholesterol.

Mousse: a frozen or chilled dish with a light, creamy texture. Traditionally it is composed of a flavored base aerated with beaten egg whites, whipped cream or both.

Navel orange: a seedless orange characterized by the navel-like indentation opposite its stem end. It is particularly easy to peel and segment.

Nonreactive pan or bowl: a cooking vessel whose surface does not react chemically with the acids in food. Ovenproof clay, stainless steel, enamel, glass and nonstick-coated aluminum are all considered nonreactive materials.

Papaya (also called pawpaw): a pear-shaped, melonlike tropical fruit rich in vitamins A and C. Like mango, it may cause an allergic reaction in some individuals.

Parchment paper: a reusable paper treated with silicon to produce a nonstick surface. It is used to line cake pans and baking sheets, and to wrap foods for baking.

Passion fruit: a juicy, fragrant, egg-shaped tropical fruit with wrinkled skin, yellow flesh and many small black seeds. The seeds are edible; the skin is not.

Plantain: a starchy variety of banana that is normally cooked before it is eaten. Although the skin turns yellowish brown and then black as the plantain ripens, the flesh remains creamy yellow or slightly pink.

Phyllo: a paper-thin pastry used notably in Greek and Turkish cuisine. Because frozen phyllo dries out easily, it should be defrosted in the refrigerator, and any phyllo sheets not in use should be covered with a damp towel.

Poach: to cook a food in barely simmering liquid as a means of preserving moisture and adding flavor. Fruit may be poached in wine or a light syrup.

Polyunsaturated fat: one of three types of fatty acid found in fats. Polyunsaturated fats, which exist in abundance in safflower and other vegetable oils, lower the level of cholesterol in the blood.

Poppy seeds: the spherical black seeds produced by a variety of poppy plant, and used as an ingredient or topping in cookies and cakes. Poppy seeds are so small that one pound of them numbers nearly a million seeds.

Purée: to reduce food to a smooth consistency by mashing it, forcing it through a sieve, or processing it in a food processor or a blender.

Ramekin: a small, straight-sided glass or porcelain mold that is used to hold a single portion of food.

Recommended Dietary Allowance (RDA): the average daily amount of an essential nutrient as determined for groups of healthy people of various ages by the National Research Council.

Reduce: to boil down a liquid in order to concentrate its flavor or thicken its consistency.

Ricotta cheese: a creamy, white Italian cheese made from whey. In the United States, it is made from whey and milk. One cup of part-skim ricotta cheese contains 19 grams of total fat.

Rolled oats: a cereal made from oats that have been ground into meal, then steamed, rolled into flakes and dried.

Ruby port: a ruby-colored sweet dessert wine, origi-nally from the Portuguese seacoast town of Oporto, fortified with a small amount of brandy and usually aged in wood casks.

Sabayon: a foamy sauce made by beating eggs with a liquid, such as wine, over heat. A sweetened sa-bayon often serves as a topping for fruit gratins.

Safflower oil: the vegetable oil that contains the highest proportion of polyunsaturated fats.

Saturated fat: one of three types of fatty acid found in fats. Saturated fats tend to raise the level of cholesterol in the blood. Because high blood-cholesterol levels contribute to heart disease, saturated-fat consumption should be kept to a mini-mum — preferably less than 10 percent of the calories consumed each day.

Sauternes: a sweet, full-bodied table wine made in the Sauternes district of France. The best Sauternes are among the longest-lived and most expensive of French wines; domestic sauternes, however, are quite suitable for use in cooking.

Sherbet: a frozen dessert made with fruit purée or juice, sugar, water and some milk fat. It may also con-tain egg white.

Sodium: a nutrient that is essential to maintaining the proper balance of fluids in the body. In most diets, a major source of the element is table salt, which contains 40 percent sodium. Excess sodium may contribute to high blood pressure, which in-creases the risk of heart disease. One teaspoon of salt, with about 2,100 milligrams of sodium, contains about two thirds of the maximum "safe and ade-quate" daily sodium intake recommended by the National Research Council.

Sorbet: a frozen mixture of fruit purée or juice, sugar and often water that may be served as a dessert or as a refreshing interlude between courses. It may also contain egg white.

Spring-form pan: a round pan with removable sides, designed to hold desserts, such as cheesecake, that cannot be unmolded.

Stone-ground cornmeal: a coarse corn flour milled by the older method that crushes grain between stones that revolve slowly and stay cool, thus preserv-ing nutrients. Though yellow and white cornmeal have similar baking properties, the yellow variety con-tains more vitamin A.

Streusel: a filling or topping for desserts, usually made by combining flour, butter, sugar and flavor-ings to form coarse crumbs.

Tapioca: an easily digestible starch derived from the fleshy root of a tropical plant. Tapioca thickens when it is heated in liquid.

Terrine: a loaf-shaped earthenware casserole, or the delicacy that is cooked in one.

Timbale: a small, usually drum-shaped baking dish or its contents.

Torte: classically, a rich cake with crumbs or ground nuts replacing all or part of the flour. The lighter ver-sion in this book calls for sherbet and meringue.

Total fat: an individual's daily intake of polyunsat-urated, monounsaturated and saturated fats. Nutri-tionists recommend that total fat constitute no more than 30 percent of the calories in a diet. The term as used in the nutrient analyses in this book refers to all the sources of fat in a recipe.

Unbleached all-purpose flour: a versatile blend of hard and soft wheat flours that is finer than bread flour but coarser than cake flour. Bleached and un-bleached flours may be used virtually interchange-ably, although slightly more liquid is needed in rec-ipes calling for the unbleached kind since it absorbs liquid more readily.

Vanilla bean: the fermented and cured pod of a climbing orchid, native to Central America, used to flavor desserts. The whole pod may be steeped in a liquid, or the pod may be split and the tiny black seeds inside scraped out for use as the flavoring.

Vanilla extract, pure: the flavoring extracted by macerating vanilla pods in an alcohol solution. Artifi-cial vanilla is chemically synthesized from clove oil.

White peppercorns: the dried cores of fully ripened berries harvested from the tropical pepper vine. White peppercorns are milder than black pepper-corns; many cooks prefer them for light-colored foods and sauces.

Yogurt: a smooth-textured, semisolid cultured-milk product. Yogurt may be frozen with fruit and eaten as a dessert. It can also substitute for sour cream in cooking or be combined with sour cream to produce a sauce or topping that is lower in fat and calories than sour cream alone.

Zest: the flavorful outermost layer of citrus-fruit rind; it should be cut or grated free of the white pith that lies beneath it.

Index

Almond cookies (amaretti), 110
Almond cream, blackberry timbales
    with, 93
Almonds:
    Candied, apple sorbet with, 47
    Meringues, 66
    Tartlets, gingery, with peaches and,
        119
Amaretti, 110
Amaretto flan with plum sauce, 79
Angel-food cake, marbled, 104
Apples:
    Baked
        filled with cranberries and golden
            raisins, 131
        filled with grapes, 41
    Brown Betty with Cheddar cheese,
        39
    Buckwheat crepes filled with, and
        cider syrup, 100
    Glazed nuggets, maple mousse
        with, 83
    Iced mousse cake with brandy snaps,
        61
    Sorbet with candied almonds, 47
    Timbales with prunes, and lemon
        syrup, 23
Applesauce, rhubarb, with sugar toast,
    136
Apricots:
    Poached, in caramel-orange sauce,
        13
    Sauce, ricotta-stuffed pears in, 34
    Vanilla custard with yogurt and, 131
Avocado ice milk, bombe of grapefruit
    and, with candied zest, 74

Bananas:
    Flan, 84
    Oranges and
        in chocolate puffs, 115
        flowers of, with caramel sauce, 14
    Yogurt, frozen, with streusel
        crumbs, 60
Batter, buckwheat crepe, 100
    Sauternes crepe, 122
Bavarian, layered, 87
Beet-orange cake, 102
Berries. See also individual names
    Cobbler, 33
    Meringue baskets filled with, 124
    Sauce, poached peaches with, 25
Blackberries:
    French cream cheese with, 82
    Timbales with almond cream, 93
Blueberries:
    With dumpling topping, 128
    Filling, cornmeal tartlets with, 120
    Lemon mousse, chilled, with, 85
    Peaches and, with crumble topping,
        27
    Sauce, lemon cornmeal cake with,
        116

Sorbet, 46
Bombe, avocado and grapefruit, with
    candied zest, 74
Bourbon chocolate squares, 127
Brandy snaps, 111
    Iced apple mousse cake with, 61
Brown Betty, apple, with Cheddar
    cheese, 39
Buckwheat crepes, apple-filled, with
    cider syrup, 100
Buttermilk:
    Cake, honey-glazed, 101
    Cream, Indian pudding with, 95
    Lemon custard with, and candied
        lemon slices, 80
    Orange parfaits with, 88

Cakes:
    Angel-food, marbled, 104
    Bourbon chocolate squares, 127
    Buttermilk, honey-glazed, 101
    Cheesecakes
        orange chiffon, 96
        raisin, 92
    Cherry-walnut, rolled, 124
    Chocolate chiffon, with raspberry
        filling, 105
    Chocolate pudding, 129
    Iced apple mousse, with brandy
        snaps, 61
    Lemon cornmeal, with blueberry
        sauce, 116
    Orange-beet, 102
    Rhubarb-gingerbread upside-down,
        136
    Tangerine chiffon, with lemon glaze,
        116
Cake topping, 36
Candied almonds, apple sorbet with,
    47
Candied lemon slices, lemon-
    buttermilk custard with, 80
Candied zest, 75
    Avocado and grapefruit bombe
        with, 74
Cantaloupe:
    Ice with poppy seeds and port sauce,
        62
    And papayas in sweet jalapeño
        sauce, 15
    Strawberries and, in fruit jelly, 43
Cappuccino parfaits, 63
Caramel-orange sauce, poached
    apricots in, 13
Caramel sauce, orange-banana flowers
    with, 14
Cassis sauce, fig flowers with, 17
Champagne:
    Jelly with grapes, 42
    Peaches with mint and, 18
    Raspberry sauce with, 105
    Sorbet of strawberries and, 57
Cheddar cheese, apple brown Betty
    with, 39

Cheese:
    Cheddar, apple brown Betty with, 39
    Cream, French, with blackberries, 82
    Cream filling, 118
    Ricotta
        filling, 115
        pears stuffed with, in apricot
            sauce, 34
Cheesecakes:
    Orange chiffon, 96
    Raisin, 92
Cherries:
    Black Forest, 24
    Filling, rolled walnut cake with, 124
    Ice cream, 74
    Pitting, 24
    Puffs, 103
Chiffon cakes:
    Chocolate, with raspberry filling,
        105
    Orange cheesecake, 96
    Tangerine, with lemon glaze, 116
Chilies:
    Cautionary note on, 15
    Jalapeño sauce, sweet, papayas and
        cantaloupe in, 15
Chocolate:
    Bourbon squares, 127
    Chiffon cake with raspberry filling,
        105
    Custards, baked, 78
    Leaves, 35
    Mocha pudding, 133
    Oatmeal-cocoa kisses, 109
    Pudding cake, 129
    Puffs, bananas and oranges in, 115
Chou-puff dough, 103
Cider syrup, apple-filled buckwheat
    crepes with, 100
Cigarettes (cookies), 113
    Shaping, 112
Cinnamon topping, 97
Citrus fruit. See also individual names
    Cups from, cutting, 52
    Segmenting, 14
    Zest, candied, 75
        avocado and grapefruit bombe
            with, 74
Cobblers:
    Berry, mixed, 33
    Nectarine, 36
Cocoa and chocolate. See Chocolate
Coconut quills, papaya porcupines
    with, 106
Coffee:
    Cappuccino parfaits, 63
    Ice cream, spiced, 70
    Mocha pudding, 133
    Soufflé, 132
Compotes:
    Apple-prune, in timbales with lemon
        syrup, 23
    Tropical fruit, with rum, 28
Cookies:
    Amaretti, 110

Brandy snaps, 111
    iced apple mousse cake with, 61
Fig bars, 114
Oatmeal, crisp, 109
Oatmeal-cocoa kisses, 109
Shaped, 112-113
Cornmeal:
    Cake, lemon, with blueberry sauce,
        116
    Tartlets with tapioca-blueberry
        filling, 120
Cranberries:
    Baked apples filled with golden
        raisins and, 131
    And pears, crisp of, 38
    Sauce, 90
    Sorbet, 51
Cream, plums with, 21
Cream cheese, French, with
    blackberries, 82
Cream filling, 118
Creams:
    Almond, 93
    Buttermilk, 95
    Lemon, 94
Crepe batter, buckwheat, 100
    Sauternes, 122
Crepes:
    Apple-filled buckwheat, with cider
        syrup, 100
    With glazed pears, 122
Crisp, pear and cranberry, 38
Crumble, blueberry-peach, 27
Crumble topping, 27
Cups, fruit, cutting, 52
Custards:
    Amaretto flan with plum sauce, 79
    Banana flan, 84
    Chocolate, baked, 78
    Lemon-buttermilk, with candied
        lemon slices, 80
    Maple, with walnuts, 135
    Vanilla, with yogurt and apricots, 131

Date-ginger ice cream, 73
Desserts, 6-7, 9, 77. See also Custards;
    Frozen desserts; Fruit desserts;
    Microwave desserts; Mousses;
    Pastry desserts; Puddings; Yogurt
Bavarian, layered, 87
Cheesecakes
    orange chiffon, 96
    raisin, 92
French cream cheese with
    blackberries, 82
Garnishes for
    candied citrus zest, 75
    chocolate leaves, 35
Ingredients for, 6-7, 9
Nutritional aspects of, 6, 7, 8
Parfaits
    cappuccino, 63
    orange and buttermilk, 88
Pie, mile-high, with two sauces, 90

Serving, 9
Soufflés
   coffee, 132
   raspberry, 89
Timbales
   apple-prune, with lemon syrup, 23
   blackberry, with almond cream, 93
Dietary considerations, 6, 7, 8, *chart* 8
Dough, chou-puff, 103
Dumpling topping, fresh blueberries with, 128

Egg whites, use of, 9
   Folding, 95

Fats in desserts, 6
Figs:
   Bars, 114
   Flowers with cassis sauce, 17
   And raspberries brûlées, 40
Filberts, pears with, 37
Fillings:
   Blueberry, with tapioca, 120
   Cherry, 124
   Cream, 118
   Raspberry, 105
   Ricotta, 115
   Tapioca-blueberry, 120
Flans:
   Amaretto, with plum sauce, 79
   Banana, 84
Folding mixtures, 95
Food processor, use of, for frozen desserts, 46
Freezing desserts, 45,46
Frozen desserts, 45-75
   Apple mousse cake, iced, with brandy snaps, 61
   Apple sorbet with candied almonds, 47
   Avocado and grapefruit bombe with candied zest, 74
   Banana yogurt with streusel crumbs, 60
   Blueberry sorbet, 46
   Cappuccino parfaits, 63
   Cherry ice cream, 74
   Coffee ice cream, spiced, 70
   Cranberry sorbet, 51
   Freezing, 45, 46
   Gewürztraminer sorbet with frosted grapes, 55
   Gin and pink grapefruit sorbet, 56
   Ginger-date ice cream, 73
   Grape pops, 68
   Kiwi sorbet, 50
   Lemon cups, 49
   Lemon-meringue torte, 66
   Lime cups, 49
   Mango ice cream, 69

Melon ice with poppy seeds and port sauce, 62
Mint julep ice, 55
Nectarine and plum terrine, 67
Orange and passion fruit cups, 52
Peach ice cream, 72
Peach yogurt, 59
Piña coladas, 64
Plum and red wine sorbet with raisin sauce, 53
Raspberry yogurt, 59
Strawberry and Champagne sorbet, 57
Strawberry ice cream, 71
Vanilla yogurt, 59
Watermelon sorbet, sliced, 65
Fruit desserts, 7, 11-43. *See also individual names*
   Berries
      cobbler, 33
      meringue baskets filled with, 124
      sauce, 25
   Citrus
      cups from, cutting, 52
      segmenting, 14
      zest, candied, 75
   Compote, tropical, with rum, 28
   Dried, kugel with, 97
   In ginger syrup, 17
   Jelly, strawberries and melon in, 43
   Phyllo roll filled with nuts and, 123
   Salad, summer, 22
   Selecting, 7, 9
   Tartlets, glazed, 118

Garnishes:
   Candied citrus zest, 75
   Chocolate leaves, 35
Gewürztraminer sorbet with frosted grapes, 55
Gin and pink grapefruit sorbet, 56
Ginger:
   Ice cream with dates, 73
   Peach and almond tartlets with, 119
   Syrup, fresh fruit in, 17
Gingerbread-rhubarb upside-down cake, 136
Glazed apple nuggets, maple mousse with, 83
Glazed fruit tartlets, 118
Glazed pears, crepes with, 122
Glazes:
   Honey, 101
   Lemon, 116
Grand Marnier, grapefruit with, 19
Grapefruit. *See also* Citrus fruit
   Bombe of avocado and, with candied zest, 74
   With Grand Marnier, 19
   Sorbet, 74
      gin and pink grapefruit, 56
Grapes:
   Baked apples filled with, 41
   Champagne jelly with, 42

Frosted, Gewürztraminer sorbet with, 55
Pops, frozen, 68

Honey-glazed buttermilk cake, 101
Honey in desserts, 7

Ice cream:
   Cherry, 74
   Coffee, spiced, 70
   Freezing methods for, 46
   Ginger-date, 73
   Mango, 69
   Peach, 72
   Strawberry, 71
Ice milk, avocado, 74
Ices. *See also* Sherbet; Sorbets
   Melon, with poppy seeds and port sauce, 62
   Mint julep, 55
Indian pudding with buttermilk cream, 95
Italian meringue, 87

Jalapeño sauce, sweet, papayas and cantaloupe in, 15
Jelly:
   Champagne, with grapes, 42
   Fruit, strawberries and melon in, 43

Kiwi fruits:
   Rum-soused plantains with oranges and, 26
   Sorbet, 50
Kugel with dried fruit, 97

Leaves:
   Chocolate, 35
   Cookies, 113
Lemon. *See also* Citrus fruit
   Buttermilk custard with, and candied lemon slices, 80
   Cornmeal cake with, and blueberry sauce, 116
   Cream, spiced pumpkin mousse with, 94
   Cups, 49
   Glaze, tangerine chiffon cake with, 116
   Mousse, chilled, with blueberries, 85
   Slices, candied, lemon-buttermilk custard with, 80
   Strawberry sauce with, and strawberries, 21
   Syrup, apple-prune timbales with, 23
   Torte, frozen, with meringues, 66
Lime cups, 49

Frosted, Gewürztraminer sorbet with, 55
Pops, frozen, 68

Mangoes:
   Ice cream, 69
   Preparing, 29
Maple:
   Custard with walnuts, 135
   Mousse with glazed apple nuggets, 83
Marbled angel-food cake, 104
Melon:
   Cantaloupe and papayas in sweet jalapeño sauce, 15
   Ice with poppy seeds and port sauce, 62
   Strawberries and, in fruit jelly, 43
   Watermelon sorbet, sliced, 65
Meringue:
   Almond, 66
   Baskets, berry-filled, 124
   Italian, 87
   Rhubarb tartlets topped with, 107
Microwave desserts, 127-137
   Baked apples filled with cranberries and golden raisins, 131
   Blueberries with dumpling topping, 128
   Bourbon chocolate squares, 127
   Chocolate pudding cake, 129
   Coffee soufflé, 132
   Maple custard with walnuts, 135
   Mocha pudding, 133
   Rhubarb applesauce with sugar toast, 136
   Rhubarb-gingerbread upside-down cake, 136
   Tapioca-rum pudding with orange, 134
   Vanilla custard with yogurt and apricots, 131
Mile-high pie with two sauces, 90
Mint:
   Ice, mint julep, 55
   Peaches with Champagne and, 18
Mocha pudding, 133
Mousses:
   Apple, iced cake of, with brandy snaps, 61
   Lemon, chilled, with blueberries, 85
   Maple, with glazed apple nuggets, 83
   Raspberry, 85
   Spiced pumpkin, and lemon cream, 94

Nectarines:
   Cobbler, 36
   Frozen terrine of plums and, 67
   Sorbet, 67
Noodle pudding (kugel) with dried fruit, 97
Nutritional considerations, 6, 7, 8, *chart* 8
Nuts:
   Almonds
      candied, apple sorbet with, 47
      meringues, 66

tartlets, gingery, with peaches
and, 119
Filberts, pears with, 37
Phyllo roll filled with fruit and, 123
Walnuts
cake, rolled, with cherries, 124
crust, spiced, pears with, 120
maple custard with, 135

*O*ak leaves (cookies), 113
Oatmeal:
Cookies
and cocoa kisses, 109
crisp, 109
Toppings, 33, 38
Orange: *See also* Citrus fruit
Bananas and
in chocolate puffs, 115
flowers of, with caramel sauce, 14
Cake with beets, 102
Caramel sauce with, poached
apricots in, 13
Cheesecake, chiffon, 96
Chiffon cake with lemon glaze, 116
Cups from, cutting, 52
Cups with passion fruit, 52
Macerated in red wine and port, 12
Parfaits with buttermilk, 88
Rum-soused plantains with kiwi
fruits and, 26
Segmenting, 14
Tapioca-rum pudding with, 134

*P*apayas:
And cantaloupe in sweet jalapeño
sauce, 15
Porcupines with coconut quills,
106
Parfaits:
Cappuccino, 63
Orange and buttermilk, 88
Passion fruit and orange cups, 52
Pastry desserts, 99-125
Cakes
angel-food, marbled, 104
bourbon chocolate squares, 127
buttermilk, honey-glazed, 101
cherry-walnut, rolled, 124
chocolate chiffon, with raspberry
filling, 105
chocolate pudding, 129
lemon cornmeal, with blueberry
sauce, 116
orange-beet, 102
rhubarb-gingerbread upside-
down, 136
tangerine chiffon, with lemon
glaze, 116
Cookies
amaretti, 110
brandy snaps, 111
fig bars, 114
oatmeal, crisp, 109

oatmeal-cocoa kisses, 109
shaped, 112-113
Crepes
apple-filled buckwheat, with cider
syrup, 100
with glazed pears, 122
Meringue baskets, berry-filled, 124
Papaya porcupines with coconut
quills, 106
Phyllo roll, fruit-and-nut-filled, 123
Puffs
cherry, 103
chocolate, bananas and oranges
in, 115
Tart, pear, with walnut crust, 120
Tartlets
cornmeal, with tapioca-blueberry
filling, 120
gingery peach and almond, 119
glazed fruit, 118
molds, lining, with dough, 119
rhubarb, with meringue, 107
Peaches:
Blueberries and, with crumble
topping, 27
Ice cream, 72
With mint and Champagne, 18
Poached, with berry sauce, 25
Tartlets, gingery, with almonds and,
119
Yogurt, frozen, 59
Pears:
And cranberries, crisp of, 38
With filberts, 37
Glazed, crepes with, 122
Peppercorn, in sabayon sauce, 20
Ricotta-stuffed, in apricot sauce, 34
With spiced walnut crust, 120
Strawberry blossoms with red-wine
sauce and, 30
Peppercorn pears in sabayon sauce, 20
Peppers, chili:
Cautionary note on, 15
Jalapeño sauce, sweet, papayas and
cantaloupe in, 15
Phyllo dough:
Rhubarb tartlets topped with
meringue, 107
Roll, fruit-and-nut-filled, 123
Pie, mile-high, with two sauces, 90
Piña coladas, frozen, 64
Pineapple:
Gratin, 31
Peeling and slicing, 28
Pitting cherries, 24
Plantains, rum-soused, with oranges
and kiwi fruits, 26
Plums:
Baked, with streusel topping, 32
With cream, 21
Frozen terrine of nectarines and, 67
Sauce, amaretto flan with, 79
Sorbet, 67
Sorbet of red wine and, with raisin
sauce, 53

Poppy seeds, melon ice with port sauce
and, 62
Pops, frozen, grape, 68
Port:
Orange slices in red wine and, 12
Sauce, melon ice with poppy seeds
and, 62
Prune-apple timbales with lemon
syrup, 23
Pudding cake, chocolate, 129
Puddings:
Apple brown Betty with Cheddar
cheese, 39
Indian, with buttermilk cream, 95
Kugel with dried fruit, 97
Mocha, 133
Rice, with raspberry sauce, 81
Tapioca-rum, with orange, 134
Puffs:
Cherry, 103
Chocolate, bananas and oranges in,
115
Pumpkin mousse, spiced, with lemon
cream, 94

*R*aisins:
Baked apples with cranberries and,
131
Cheesecake, 92
Sauce, plum and red wine sorbet
with, 53
Raspberries:
And figs brûlées, 40
Filling, chocolate chiffon cake with,
105
Mousse, 85
Sauce, rice pudding with, 81
Sauce with Champagne, 105
Soufflés, 89
Yogurt, frozen, 59
Recommended Dietary Allowances,
chart 8
Red wine:
Orange slices in port and, 12
Sauce of, strawberry blossoms with
pears and, 30
Sorbet of plums and, with raisin
sauce, 53
Rhubarb:
Applesauce with sugar toast, 136
Gingerbread upside-down cake
with, 136
Tartlets topped with meringue, 107
Rice pudding with raspberry sauce, 81
Ricotta:
Filling, 115
Pears stuffed with, in apricot sauce,
34
Rum:
Plantains soused with, and oranges
and kiwi fruits, 26
Tapioca pudding with, and orange,
134
Tropical fruit compote with, 28

*S*abayon sauce, peppercorn pears in,
20
Salad, summer fruit, 22
Sauces:
Almond cream, 93
Berry, 25
cranberry, 90
raspberry-Champagne, 105
strawberry, 43
Caramel-orange, 13
Port, 62
Swirling, 91
Vanilla-yogurt, 90
Sauternes crepe batter, 122
Segmenting citrus fruit, 14
Sherbet, piña colada, 64
Sorbets:
Apple, with candied almonds, 47
Blueberry, 46
Cranberry, 51
Freezing methods for, 46
Gewürztraminer, with frosted
grapes, 55
Gin and pink grapefruit, 56
Grape, pops from, 68
Grapefruit, 74
Kiwi, 50
Lemon, torte from, 66
Lemon cups, 49
Lime cups, 49
Nectarine, 67
Orange and passion fruit cups,
52
Plum, 67
Plum and red wine, with raisin
sauce, 53
Strawberry and Champagne, 57
Watermelon, sliced, 65
Soufflés:
Coffee, 132
Raspberry, 89
Spiced coffee ice cream, 70
Spiced pumpkin mousse with lemon
cream, 94
Spiced walnut crust, pears with,
120
Strawberries:
Blossoms with pears and red-wine
sauce, 30
French cream cheese with, 82
Ice cream, 71
With lemon-strawberry sauce, 21
Melon and, in fruit jelly, 43
Sauce, 43
lemon-strawberry, 21
Sorbet of Champagne and, 57
Streusel:
Crumbs, frozen banana yogurt with,
60
Topping, baked plums with, 32
Sugar in desserts, 6-7
Sugar toast, rhubarb applesauce with,
136
Sweeteners in desserts, 6-7

Tangerine chiffon cake with lemon glaze, 116

Tapioca:
  Blueberry filling, cornmeal tartlets with, 120
  Rum pudding with orange, 134

Tart, pear, with spiced walnut crust, 120

Tartlets:
  Cornmeal, with tapioca-blueberry filling, 120
  Gingery peach and almond, 119
  Glazed fruit, 118
  Molds, lining, with dough, 119
  Rhubarb, topped with meringue, 107

Terrine, frozen nectarine and plum, 67

Timbales:
  Apple-prune, with lemon syrup, 23
  Blackberry, with almond cream, 93

Toast, sugar, rhubarb applesauce with, 136

Toppings:
  Cake, 36
  Cinnamon, 97
  Crumble, 27
  Dumpling, 128
  Oat, 38
  Oatmeal, 33
  Streusel, 32

Torte, frozen lemon-meringue, 66

Tulipes (cookies), 113
  Shaping, 112

Upside-down cake, rhubarb-gingerbread, 136

Vanilla:
  Custard with yogurt and apricots, 131
  Yogurt, frozen, 59
  Yogurt sauce with, 90

Walnuts:
  Cake, rolled, with cherries, 124
  Crust, spiced, pears with, 120
  Maple custard with, 135

Watermelon sorbet, sliced, 65

Wine:
  Champagne
    jelly with grapes, 42
    peaches with mint and, 18
    raspberry sauce with, 105
    sorbet of strawberries and, 57
  Gewürztraminer sorbet with frosted grapes, 55
  Port
    orange slices macerated in red wine and, 12
    sauce, 62
  Red
    orange slices macerated in port and, 12
    sauce of, strawberry blossoms with pears and, 30
    sorbet of plums and, with raisin sauce, 53

Sauternes crepe batter, 122

Yogurt:
  Frozen
    banana, with streusel crumbs, 60
    peach, 59
    raspberry, 59
    vanilla, 59
  Homemade, 92
  Sauce with vanilla, 90
  Vanilla custard with apricots and, 131

Zest, candied, 75
  Avocado and grapefruit bombe with, 74

Picture Credits

All photographs in this book were taken by staff photographer Renée Comet unless otherwise indicated:

2: top, Scarlet Cheng; center, Carolyn Wall Rothery. 4: lower left, Rina Ganassa. 5: upper right, Michael Latil. 6: courtesy Harris Country Heritage Society, Houston, Tex. 14: top, Lisa Masson; bottom, Michael Latil. 15-17: Lisa Masson. 19: Lisa Masson. 21: Lisa Masson. 23: Lisa Masson. 24: right, Taran Z. 26: Rina Ganassa. 28: Taran Z. 29: bottom, Michael Latil. 30: Michael Latil. 32: Lisa Masson. 34: Lisa Masson. 35: Taran Z. 37, 38: Lisa Masson. 52: bottom, Michael Latil. 86: Rina Ganassa. 87: Michael Latil. 91: Michael Latil. 95: top, Michael Latil. 100-103: Michael Latil. 105, 106: Michael Latil. 108: Michael Latil. 110: Michael Latil. 112-113: techniques, Taran Z; cookies, Michael Latil. 114, 115: Michael Latil. 118: Michael Latil. 119: top, Taran Z; bottom, Michael Latil. 120, 121: Michael Latil. 124: Michael Latil. 126: Michael Latil. 128: Michael Latil. 131: Michael Latil. 135: Steven Biver.

Props: Cover: Cowdy Glass Studio, Rogers-Tropea, Inc., New York. 12: Royal Worcester Spode Inc., New York; flatware, Retroneu, New York. 13: Elayne De Vito. 14: Tayo Gabler by Margaret Chatelain, Bristol, Vt. 15: Williams-Sonoma, Washington, D.C. 16: Art Reed, The Glass Gallery, Bethesda, Md.; flatware, Retroneu. 17: Annieglass, Santa Cruz, Calif.; flatware, Retroneu. 18: Margaret Chatelain. 19: Jon Choy. 20: Mark Anderson, Torpedo Factory Art Center, Alexandria, Va. 21: top, William Gudenrath, New York; bottom, Williams-Sonoma, Alexandria, Va. 23: Limor Carrigan, Crofton, Md. 24: saucepan, Williams-Sonoma. 25: Marc Western Decorative Arts, Washington, D.C. 27: Sharon Farrington. 29: Javier Bellosillo for Swid Powell, The American Hand Plus, Washington, D.C. 33: hand-painted napkin, Heleen Heyning, Creative Resources, Inc., New York. 34: Martin's of Georgetown, Washington, D.C. 37: Nambé Mills, Inc., Santa Fe, N. Mex. 38: Kathryn Berd Ceramics, Seattle, Wash. 39: The Hall China Co., East Liverpool, Ohio. 40: Hulda's Antiques, Alexandria, Va. 41: Judith K. Zieve, Helen Drutt Gallery, Philadelphia, Pa. 42: King's Jewelry, Alexandria, Va. 44-45: Antiques and Art Plus, Vienna, Va. 46: Preferred Stock, Washington, D.C.; spoons, David Tisdale, Rogers-Tropea, Inc. 51: Yetta Cohen. 52: Blue Moon, Washington, D.C. 53: Little Caledonia Inc., Washington, D.C. 54: racing colors, Becker & Durski Manufacturing Co., Louisville, Ky. 56: Gertrude Berman. 58: Cowdy Glass Studio, Rogers-Tropea, Inc. 59: Kathy Erteman, Rogers-Tropea, Inc. 61: Nambé Mills, Inc.; tablecloth, Gertrude Berman. 62: Williams-Sonoma; napkins, A Bit of Britain, Alexandria, Va. 63: Shirley E. Cherkasky. 66: Cambet de France, Washington, D.C. 67: Rob Barnard, Timberville, Va. 69: Chenonceau Antiques, Washington, D.C. 70: Georgetown Coffee Tea and Spice, Washington, D.C. 71: Kathy Swekel. 72: Gertrude Berman. 73: scoop, Franette McCulloch. 74: Stephen Smyers, Rogers-Tropea, Inc. 76-77: wisk, Williams-Sonoma; bowl, Antiques and Art Plus. 78: Jean Wilson. 79: spoon, Lynn A. Ascher. 80: Kathleen Eggert, The Glass Gallery. 81: Skellin and Company, Bethesda, Md. 82: Ellen Godwin. 83: Jane Beecham, Fire One, Torpedo Factory Art Center. 84: flower holder, Paula Sussman. 86: Hulda's Antiques. 88: Jackie Chalkley Fine Crafts and Wearables, Washington, D.C. 89: Williams-Sonoma. 90: Shaun Weisbach, Appalachiana, Bethesda, Md. 92: Hulda's Antiques. 94: Shirley E. Cherkasky. 95: Rob Barnard. 96: Hutschenreuther Corporation, New York. 97: Michael Obronovich, Appalachian Spring, Washington, D.C. 98-99: Mabel's Kountry Store, Alexandria, Va. 100: China Closet, Bethesda, Md. 101: cake pan, Mabel's Kountry Store. 102: Pan American Phoenix, New York. 103: Skellin and Company. 104: tablecloth, Gertrude Berman. 105: Billy Goldsmith, Frank McIntosh at Stanley Korshak, Dallas, Tex.; cake server, Retroneu. 106: Jurg Lanzrein, Dolly Kay Designs, Washington, D.C. 108: plate, Ann Gordon; cookie jar, Mabel's Kountry Store. 109: canisters, Chenonceau Antiques. 110: Il Papiro, New York. 115: Cambet de France. 116: Pat Ridgeway. 117: Justine Mehlman, Georgetown Antique Center, Washington, D.C. 118: China Closet. 119: David Nelson, The American Hand Plus. 120: Judith K. Zieve, Helen Drutt Gallery. 122: Margaret Chatelain. 123: Chenonceau Antiques. 124: Irongate Antiques, Washington, D.C. 125: Terrafirma Ceramics Inc., New York. 126: Dorothy Hafner, Tiffany & Co., New York. 129: Dorothy Hafner, Dolly Kay Designs. 131: Dolly Kay Designs. 134: Strini Glass, Appalachian Spring. 136: Skellin and Company. 137: Thaxton & Co., New York.

Acknowledgments

The index for this book was prepared by Barbara Klein. The editors are particularly indebted to the following people for creating recipes for this volume: Nora Carey, Paris; Robert Chambers, New York; Carole Clements, London; Sharon Farrington, Bethesda, Md.; Rebecca Marshall, New York; Wendye Pardue, New Canaan, Conn.; Richard Spinell, Hoboken, N.J.; Peter Staehli, Gaithersburg, Md.; Kathleen Stang, Washington, D.C.; Jolene Worthington, Chicago, Ill.

The editors also wish to thank: Jo Calabrese, Royal Worcester Spode Inc., New York; Jackie Chalkley, Fine Crafts and Wearables, Washington, D.C.; Nic Colling, Home Produce Company, Alexandria, Va.; Margaret Berry Cotton, Hanover, N.H.; La Cuisine, Alexandria, Va.; Jeanne Dale, The Pilgrim Glass Corp., New York; Rex Downey, Oxon Hill, Md.; Flowers Unique, Alexandria, Va.; Flying Foods, International, Long Island City, N.Y.; Dennis Garrett, Ed Nash, The American Hand Plus, Washington, D.C.; Giant Foods, Inc., Landover, Md.; Judith Goodkind, Alexandria, Va.; Chong Su Han, Grass Roots Restaurant, Alexandria, Va.; Joe Huffer, Mount Solon, Va.; Imperial Produce, Washington, D.C.; Kitchen Bazaar, Washington, D.C.; Kossow Gourmet Produce, Washington, D.C.; Gary Latzman, Kirk Phillips, Retroneu, New York; Magruder's, Inc., Rockville, Md.; Sara Mark, Alexandria, Va.; Nambé Mills Inc., Santa Fe, N. Mex.; Andrew Naylor, Alexandria, Va.; Hiu Newcomb, Potomac Vegetable Farms, Vienna, Va.; Northwest Cherry Growers; Lisa Ownby, Alexandria, Va.; Joyce Piotrowski, Vienna, Va.; C. Kyle and Ruth Randall, Alexandria, Va.; Linda Robertson, JUD Tile, Vienna, Va.; Safeway Stores, Inc., Landover, Md.; Bert Saunders, WILTON Armetale, New York; Sid and Betty Solomon, Capitol Restaurant Equipment Co., Washington, D.C.; Nancy Snyder, Snyder's Sprouts, Rockville, Md.; Straight from the Crate, Inc.; Alexandria, Va.; Sutton Place Gourmet, Washington, D.C.; Kathy Swekel, Columbia, Md.; Nancy Teksten, National Onion Association, Greeley, Colo.; United Fresh Fruit and Vegetable Association, Alexandria, Va.; U.S. Fish, Kensington, Md.; Albert Uster Imports, Gaithersburg, Md.; Williams-Sonoma, Inc., Alexandria, Va.; Lynn Addison Yorke, Cheverly, Md.
The editors wish to thank the following for their donation of kitchen equipment: Le Creuset, distributed by Schiller & Asmus, Inc., Yemasse, S.C.; Cuisinarts, Inc., Greenwich, Conn.; KitchenAid, Inc., Troy, Ohio; Oster, Milwaukee, Wis.

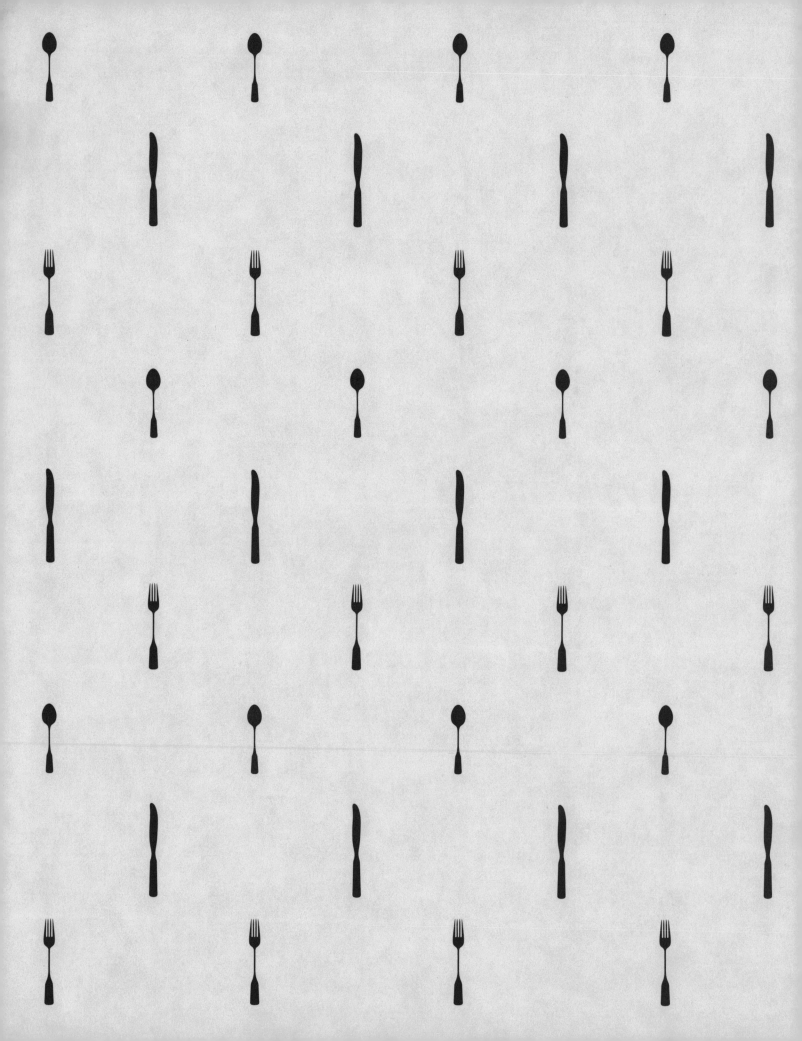